Elizabeth Ellen

Elizabeth Ellen

by Elizabeth Ellen

Short Flight / Long Drive Books
A DIVISION OF Hobart

SHORT FLIGHT/LONG DRIVE BOOKS
A division of Hobart Publishing
PO Box 1658
Ann Arbor, MI 48106
www.hobartpulp.com/minibooks

ISBN: 978-0-9896950-7-7

Printed in the United States of America

Cover art by Ian Amberson
Author photo by Elizabeth Ellen
Inside text set in Latienne Pro
Layout by Alban Fischer

For my mother, still the greatest influence on my life

And for Aaron, thank you for being my D.C.

In poetry, I don't like the worked-over language, I like the facts and ideas. I am more interested in the neutrality and anonymity of our shared language than by the attempts of poets to make a language of their own, a factual report seems to me the most beautifully unpoetic poetry there is.

—EDOUARD LEVE, *Autoportrait*

Anything I can sing, I call a song. Anything I can't sing, I call a poem. Anything I can't sing or anything that's too long to be a poem, I call a novel. But my novels don't have the usual story lines. They're about my feelings at a certain place at a certain time.

—BOB DYLAN, liner notes for *The Freewheelin' Bob Dylan*

I wouldn't publish these marriage poems if I were you. Only ▮▮▮ emerges unscathed.

—ANONYMOUS WRITER FRIEND, upon reading these poems

That is one last thing to remember: *writers are always selling somebody out.*

—JOAN DIDION, Preface, *Slouching Towards Bethlehem*

Contents

BOB DYLAN SONGS *(June, 2016 - November, 2016)*

'90S RIOT GRRRLS SONGS *(September, 2016 - December, 2016)*

Elizabeth Ellen

NICKI MINAJ SONGS

(May, 2015 – August, 2015)

My Daughter Is a Science Major

I think that makes me a feminist

Mother's Day

We were at a baseball game.

I said, "We are strong independent women because we are at a baseball game without
men."

My daughter said, "Mmmmhmmm."

We were standing over a trashcan eating pizza out of boxes.

The trashcan was our dinner table.

People said "excuse me" when they threw their trash in our dinner table.

When it stopped raining we went back to our seats.

The woman in front of us was talking about a reality tv show.

The woman was speaking very loud to a man who seemed hard of hearing or interested in
the game or something.

The woman used the term "slut-shaming" to refer to some aspect of the show she didn't
like but didn't stop her from watching the show.

I had never given the term much thought but now I had more time on my hands.

"Is it just me, or is the term 'slut-shaming' offensive to women?" I asked my daughter.

"I mean," I said. "You wouldn't use the term 'nigger-shaming.'"

"Right," my daughter said. "Or 'faggot-shaming.'"

"So why do women think it's okay to say 'slut-shaming'?"

"Maybe they should start saying something like, 'sexually confident women shaming' or
'women who don't give a fuck shaming,'" I said.

"It's hard to shame a woman who doesn't give a fuck," my daughter said.

"True," I said.

"Women should just stop giving a fuck," my daughter said.

"No one gave a fuck when Chris fucked Brit," I said.

"What?" my daughter said. She didn't watch *The Bachelor*.

"Nothing," I said.

On the drive home it was raining and my daughter's GPS told us to go a way I didn't want
to go.

I went my way instead.

We ended up going south when we wanted to go north.

I had to keep making turns to try to go north.

Part of me thought we might be lost but the other part of me said to just keep making turns.

"I don't know if I want to do marine biology anymore," my daughter said.

"I think I might want to do forensic science instead."

It was pouring and I could barely make out the car in front of me
But I didn't pull over.
I turned on my hazards and gripped the wheel with both hands and kept going.

My Best Friend Growing Up Had a Sticker on Her Car That Said 'Party Naked'

We were playing a late night party game after the rest of the party guests had gone
     home—Me and Tanja and Tanja's boyfriend and my husband—
Tanja said, "Okay, what's your deepest regret?"
I looked at Tanja.
Tanja was looking at my husband.
I looked at my husband.
He was reclined in a chair with our dog.
Tanja and Tanja's boyfriend and I were all seated around the same round table.
My husband started to say something and then stopped.
Tanja and her boyfriend told people they had been together—"off and on"—
Six years.
My husband and I had been together—"off and on"—for thirteen.
We had just celebrated our fourth anniversary.
We were living in separate houses in the same city.
Sometimes that summer we had worn our wedding bands and sometimes we hadn't.
I was wearing mine now but I wouldn't be wearing it tomorrow.
"Don't think, just answer," Tanja said.
"Well," my husband said.
I could see what he was thinking; he was thinking his deepest regret was marrying me.
I couldn't make out if he was wearing his wedding band or not.
Tanja thought I was kidding.
"You guys are just joking," Tanja said.
"No," my husband said. "She's right. That was what I was going to say."
I don't know why but I wasn't that bothered by my husband's answer.
"It doesn't bother me that much," I said to Tanja.
"Maybe we're just super honest with each other," I said.
"How honest are you guys with each other?" I asked Tanja.
Tanja looked at her boyfriend.
Tanja said, "I don't know."
Later Tanja's boyfriend kept saying "are you mad?" to Tanja.
Tanja's boyfriend seemed to worry about Tanja being mad a lot.
My husband was falling asleep.
My husband got up and went to bed.
Tanja and Tanja's boyfriend and I were still sitting at the table.
In an hour I would get in bed next to my husband.
The night after that I would get into bed alone.
It didn't bother me that much.
I'd stopped worrying if my husband was mad at me.
It didn't seem like he worried anymore either.

Beyoncé Knowles (Wears Nike Kneepads)

Are you Beyoncé? My daughter says.
I am holding a pair of Nike kneepads in my hand.
No, I say.
I am not Beyoncé, I say.
My daughter doesn't say anything else.
My daughter makes a certain face, raises her hand open palm in front of her.
This means 'exactly.'
My daughter means, '*exactly*, you are *not* Beyoncé.'

I wait until my daughter has left the room to put on the Nike kneepads

I stand on a chair in the middle of my room
I spin while my hands are up
I clap clap clap like I don't care
I dance down the hallway with a pretend cup in my hand
I hold that coke like alcohol
I wave my hands from side to side,
I am careful not to drop the alcohol
I dance in front of my bathroom mirror
I move my legs from side to side,
I smack it in the air
I clap clap clap like I don't care

I forget for a minute I am not Beyoncé
(Inside I think maybe we are all Beyoncé)

I think, *my daughter is mad cause I'm so fresh*
I think, *I'm fresher than you*, and by 'you' I mean my daughter, but also I mean everyone
    else I have ever met

afterward I put the Nike kneepads in a drawer in my closet so my daughter will not find
    them

I don't ever again want to be told I am not Beyoncé

SNL

Nicki Minaj just said, "all my independent women make some noise."
I didn't know if she meant me.
I was still alone in this hotel room.
It was almost one in the morning.

I said, 'heyyyyy' real soft in case the person in the adjoining room was sleeping.

Then I went back to writing these poems.

Target

I went to Target to buy the new Kid Rock CD.
The woman who rang me up was young and black.
She said, "Oh, he's still putting out albums?"

She was smiling in a genuine way. I felt like we liked each other even though she was
    teasing me about Kid Rock.

I said, "Yeah, this is his new one, it just came out."
"Didn't he have some sort of . . . *trouble* . . . with Beyoncé?" she said.
"Did he?" I said. My mind was blank.
"Yeah," she said. "You can't mess with Beyoncé or Rihanna, their people will get you
    on Twitter."

She was still smiling. I still felt good about us.
"Right," I said. I was smiling too.

I seemed to remember something about Kid Rock and Beyoncé but then I forget it again.

She handed me my receipt and I started to walk away when I remembered something.

"Hey," I said. "I just remembered I'm wearing my Beyoncé shirt." I started unzipping my
    jacket to show her. She walked toward me to look. The shirt was red and long sleeved
    and said, "all I'm really asking for is you" and under that is said, "Beyoncé."

"Oh, yeah," she said. We were still smiling even though we had nothing more to say.

Broad City

I was sitting on the futon in my daughter's dorm room. My daughter was in the bathroom. We were watching *Broad City*.

My daughter's roommate came in from class.

She stood watching the TV a minute. She had a confused look on her face. She said, "Did they purposely pick the plainest women they could find for this show."

"They created the show and write it," I said.

"Oh," her roommate said.

Benson & Hedges

It was a three mile walk and I walked the three miles listening to one song on repeat.
It was a song I liked but I liked not having to think about what other songs to play also.
I walked in avoidance of other people, men in particular.
I crossed the street if someone was coming toward me.
I tried to go around a house to avoid a group of construction workers but when I got to the side of the house there was a fence and I couldn't climb the fence so I had to return to the side of the house with the men who worked construction.
I wondered if they had noticed my attempt at avoiding them.
If they did, they didn't say anything or they didn't say anything in English so I don't know.
Halfway home there was a tobacco store next to a liquor store.
I was out of cigarettes and there were only two places in town that carried my brand and the place I usually went was on the other side of town.
I had never gone into the tobacco store by myself.
The tobacco store was run by men and only employed men and I had only seen male customers in the store.
But I didn't want to leave the house again once I was home.
I didn't want to drive across town to the party store where I normally bought my cigarettes.
I told myself I would go into the tobacco store and it would be fine.
I told myself this when I was two blocks away and then when I was a block away I started to have doubts.
I couldn't remember why strange men scared me.
I thought maybe it had something to do with my mom's boyfriend peeing with the door open when I was in high school but I wasn't sure
It could have been because of him beating her also.
I removed one of the earbuds from my ear and left the other in.
The man behind the counter had a shaved head.
My mom's boyfriend had a tattoo that said "Shirley" (the name of his ex wife) on his left arm.
My mom always made a joke that he should get "you jest" tattooed below it.
I couldn't tell if the man at the tobacco store had any tattoos.
His shirt had long sleeves.
I saw my cigarettes over his right shoulder.
There was no one else in the store.
I fingered a stack of lighters while he got my cigarettes.
I decided he was nice and now there was one less thing I was scared of.

When I got to my house I stopped at the end of the drive to check the mailbox.

I was looking through my mail, about to walk up my drive, when I saw

Two college-age boys coming down my neighbor's drive toward me.

The boys had clipboards and were wearing similar shirts.

I had a 'no soliciting' sign on the house but I was standing at the end of my drive, out of view of the sign.

If I hesitated, the boys and I would be walking up my drive at the same time.

I was already bothered by the conversation we weren't yet having.

They were getting closer and I still hadn't made a decision what to do.

At the last second I turned and walked in the opposite direction of my house.

I walked to the end of my street and made a right and then made another right onto the street that ran parallel to mine.

I spent ten minutes circling the neighborhood in avoidance of the college-age boys with clipboards.

When I finally got back to my driveway I could see them walking up the driveway of my neighbor who lived four houses down.

I went inside and downstairs to my basement and even though it wasn't nighttime and I normally only smoked at night, I lit a cigarette,

Considering the fears I had overcome and those I hadn't.

Drake

We were driving back from an art museum in Detroit.
They were having an exhibition of Diego Rivera's and Frida Kahlo's work.
It was a Saturday morning and the museum was full of people.
I kept bumping into people.
I kept losing my daughter and bumping into people.

I felt more anxious with every new room we entered.
I was bumping into more and more people at the exact time Frida's work was becoming more and more personal and vulnerable and painful.

I stayed too long in the room detailing her miscarriage.
It was painful to look at (the painting) but even more painful to read about (her miscarriage; her only child with Diego; her inability to give him another; her misery at being unable to provide him (and herself) with a child, with a 'little Dieguito,' as she referenced the unborn child in letters).

I was silent most of the car ride back,
Forty-five minutes.
I was thinking of the children I would never have also.

We were nearing our exit when a Drake song came on the radio.

"Remember when you had to take the BAR exam, I drove in the snow for you," Drake said

"Isn't Drake from Canada?" my daughter said. "Shouldn't driving through snow be no big deal? Why is he trying to make it a big deal?"

I laughed. It was the first time that day.

Drake said, "I started drinking way more than I used to, people form habits like that, girl."

"God, dating Drake would be like dating a submissive," my daughter said.

I laughed again. It felt good to laugh two times so close together.

"What if you had to choose between dating Drake and dating Chris Brown?" I said.

"I wouldn't want to date either of them; neither of them are men, they're both boys," my daughter said.

"I know," I said. "But if you *had to*. If you *had to* choose one."

We were pulling into a gas station. My daughter had that look on her face. The one that says, "Please don't make me pump the gas."

I handed her my credit card.

The gas tank was on her side.

"Drake, then," she said, opening the car door. "But I'd be like, 'look, this is an open relationship; I'm not attracted to you' and he'd be like, 'ok'."

I smiled, knowing she had picked correctly.
Then I laughed, knowing I would pick Chris Brown. Or I was Chris Brown. I couldn't decide which.

It felt good not to be thinking about Frida Kahlo anymore.

Hercules

On Mondays and Tuesdays I volunteered at a therapeutic equestrian center.
For three hours each night I walked beside a horse and held a hand or my arm on the leg of a child or young adult so the child or young adult wouldn't fall off (someone else walked on the other side).
The children and young adults had a variety of mental and physical disabilities—autism, Down syndrome, cerebral palsy, brain tumor, cancer and other conditions I did not know the names of.
(We were not told the specific disease or condition of a child or young adult to protect his/ her privacy but often the child or young adult or the parent of the child or young adult mentioned it; once a girl I had been walking beside for six weeks said, "that was when I had my brain tumor removed" and that was how I found out about that.)

Mondays my last rider was Jeremiah.
Jeremiah was ten and had braces on his legs and wore thick glasses.
When he wanted to see something—like a ball or a toy horse—
I handed it to him and he held it close to his face and his eyes moved back and forth rapidly as he turned the object just as rapidly in his hands.
It was hard otherwise to tell what he could see because he didn't turn directly toward an object like the rest of us did to view it.

I didn't know what was 'wrong' with Jeremiah.
Aside from the braces and glasses, I mean.
He rocked back and forth in the saddle when he got bored and didn't hold his reins unless we reminded him and the instructor seemed to remind us to remind him a lot.

"Use your mother voice," she would say to me. "Be firm."

But I had forgotten my mother voice or I didn't know how to be firm or I didn't want to be.

"Jeremiah, pick up your reins," I would say in a voice that wasn't a whisper but wasn't firm either.

"Jeremiah!" the instructor would shout from the middle of the arena. "Pick up your reins!"

Jeremiah always picked up his reins when the instructor yelled and then immediately dropped them again after we passed her. Then Jeremiah would ask us questions, like, "What's your name?" "How do you spell your name?" "Where did the sun go?" (Jeremiah's lesson was between eight and nine and the sun set during that time.) "Is it nighttime?" "Who is that on the brown horse?" "Can I play with Trevor (the kid on the brown horse)?" "Why can't I play with Trevor?"

I answered all of these questions when the instructor wasn't looking and told Jeremiah to sit up and pick up his reins when she was.

I had learned during Jeremiah's first lesson not to laugh at his questions even if they were funny (which they usually were).

During the first lesson Jeremiah had asked questions like, "What if the black horse ate the brown horse?" and "Can Hercules (the horse Jeremiah rode) fly to the sun and burn up?" and "What if Hercules shriveled and dried up like an old piece of Play-Doh?"

I laughed at the Play-Doh question and then Jeremiah laughed and once Jeremiah started laughing he didn't stop laughing until the instructor yelled at him to be quiet so I stopped laughing after that too.

Once Hercules farted and no one said anything and then Jeremiah said, "What did Hercules just do?" and still none of us said anything, and finally Jeremiah said, "Did Hercules pass gas?" and the horse leader said, "Yes, Jeremiah, Hercules passed gas," in a tone that I gathered meant she was glad Jeremiah had reminded us there was a polite way to say fart.

At the end of every lesson the instructor encouraged the rider to thank his/her sidewalkers and leader and to thank his/her horse.

Jeremiah would stand, one hand on Hercules, and one hand in mine, and say, "Thank you, Hercules." Then he would say, "Can I feed Hercules a carrot?"

The first time Jeremiah asked this, no one seemed to know what to say.

Finally the instructor said what she would end up saying every week when Jeremiah asked, which was, "Did you bring Hercules a carrot?"

And Jeremiah would say, "no."

And the instructor would say, "if you bring a carrot next week, you can feed it to Hercules."

Then I had to walk Jeremiah in to his mother who was sitting in the waiting room that overlooked the arena and Jeremiah would say to his mother, "Can I feed Hercules a carrot?"

The first couple of times he asked his mother this question, she looked at me for an answer. I didn't know what to say. I knew we had carrots in the refrigerator in the volunteer break room but I didn't think the instructor wanted me to say this. I didn't think the instructor really wanted Jeremiah to bring a carrot either. But I wasn't sure.

I answered Jeremiah's mother the same way the instructor had answered Jeremiah in the arena.

"Did you bring a carrot with you?" I said.

"Jeremiah, did we bring a carrot?" the mother asked Jeremiah.

"No," Jeremiah said.

"Next week we will have to remember to bring a carrot," Jeremiah's mother said.

But the next week would be the same thing. Jeremiah would ask the instructor, I would ask his mother, . . . there was never a carrot.

I decided one week that the following Monday I would bring a carrot. I would buy a bag of carrots the next time I was at the grocery store and bring the smallest one in my pocket and at the end of Jeremiah's lesson when he asked if he could feed Hercules a carrot and the instructor asked Jeremiah if he had brought a carrot to feed Hercules I would pull it out and I would be a hero.

But I kept forgetting to buy carrots. So I had to keep asking Jeremiah's mother if they had brought one. It was a painful and awkward exchange but I couldn't seem to remember to buy carrots.

I couldn't seem to remember to buy carrots and I was never going to be a hero.

Jeremiah still kept asking.

Kid Rock

My daughter was telling me a story.

"And then Kid Rock came on the radio and I told John we were going to see him later this summer and John said, 'Aren't we supposed to hate Kid Rock now or something?' and I said, 'John, come on, you're smarter than that.'"

I smiled when my daughter told me this.

For a few seconds I felt parental pride or pride in myself or pride in some intangible I couldn't quite put my finger on.

Then I remembered all the parents I knew who dressed their toddlers in Ramones t-shirts and Black Flag t-shirts, and I just felt dumb. It seemed like all parents were dumb and taking pride in anything was dumb and I was as dumb as anyone else.

But I still laughed. It was still a funny story. We were still going to see Kid Rock later in the summer.

Ayn Rand

I felt like something was missing; there were things I didn't know, holes in my education.
I went and stood in the philosophy section of Barnes & Noble.
It was the closest bookstore to my house.
Also I held no sentimental attachment to small, independently owned bookstores.
(small, independently owned bookstores had fucked me in the past)
Also I wasn't planning to buy anything anyway.

I pulled five or six books off the shelf and sat with them on the floor.
The floor was carpeted and I was near a large window.
It was a comfortable place to sit; also the chairs were all taken.
I started flipping through the books.
The books were written by men who had been dead a considerable length of time and the
      men seemed to reference each other a lot in a way that was not dissimilar to *The Bible*.

The men didn't seem to reference women except to talk about how they made good nurses
      or schoolteachers or mothers (which was similar to *The Bible*).

It was hard to take anything the men said seriously because they seemed to be talking
      only to each other (and not to me) (which was similar to *The Bible*).

Also I couldn't understand why anyone who had already accepted that there was no god,
      would bother him/herself with a debate over ethics or free will or the interpretation
      of dreams.

(but maybe I am just lazy)

The whole thing seemed an extension of religion -
An unwillingness to accept the meaninglessness of life and the irrelevancy of morality,
      which was also manmade.

(but maybe I'm just lazy)

Also, there was another book called *Great Philosophers Who Failed at Love* and it seemed
      like they all had and that didn't seem any great surprise (but then again, maybe we're
      all just lazy).

I got up and put the books back on the shelf.
(Now I knew about philosophy and there was still half a day left.)
I put my earbuds in and walked out of the store.
"Drunk in Love" was playing from when I had walked to the store earlier.

I was trying to memorize the Jay Z part.
I had looked up the lyrics online before I left the house.

Beat the box up like Mike; in '97 I bite

I listened to the song over and over on the walk home.
By the time I got to my house I could say all the words in time with Jay Z.
I liked the way it felt (in my mouth) repeating the words.
It felt like I had accomplished something.

Drake II

We were walking the dogs and I was telling my daughter how I had received a single
rejection from an agent and how I was okay with that. "I don't know why I don't
seem to have this attachment to my writing in the way most of my friends do," I said.
I told her most of my friends had sent a novel to twenty agents on average and had
gone through a period of depression during the process.

"Yeah," my daughter said. "But if you believe in something, you shouldn't let one
rejection deter you."

"Maybe I don't believe in my novel then," I said.
"I'm just happy my self-esteem doesn't seem tied to my writing," I said. (My self-esteem
seemed tied to enough already.)
"Besides," I said. "I'm perfectly content to have it published posthumously, if anyone
wants it then."

We had been walking up a hill and now we were stopped. I turned to look at my daughter.
The dogs turned to look also.

"Well, *I'm* not going to publish it posthumously," my daughter said.

"Why not?" I said. I thought maybe she meant she wouldn't want the hassle. She had seen
firsthand how much of a hassle publishing could be.

"Because I told you not to write that book in the first place," she said. "Because I don't
agree with it."

"Oh," I said.
"Okay," I said.

I realized then, in that moment, that with relation to my daughter I was Drake.
I was submissive with my daughter in a way that made me feel comfortable.
I didn't feel this comfortable with anyone else.

My daughter started walking again; we kept walking up the hill.
We didn't talk about my writing any more.
There was a pair of adolescent deer walking down someone's drive.
I felt most comfortable not talking about my writing.

We stood still and the dogs stood still; my daughter and I made noises with our mouths. The adolescent deer stared across the street at us.

The deer stared a while, then turned down the sidewalk and up another drive; my daughter and I and the dogs walked home.

Two-fer Tuesday

for Ian

I was practicing my drums.

I had practiced by watching a YouTube video called "first drum lesson" for a week and a
half. I could finally play the bass drum and the snare drum and the hi-hat all at the
same time. For a week I could only play the bass drum and the hi-hat or the snare
drum and the hi-hat or the snare drum and the bass drum but not all three at once.

It was like learning to blow a bubble. I remember practicing while throwing a basketball
in a hoop in third grade. All of a sudden I could do it (blow a bubble) and I didn't
know how it'd happened.

Anyway, I was ready to move on.
I went for a drive to 7-Eleven for a Slurpee first.
It was "Two-fer Tuesday" on the classic rock station in my car, which meant two songs by
the same artist back to back (which meant a lot of Guns N'Roses and White Stripes
and Van Halen and Pink Floyd).

I loved "Two-fer Tuesdays." (Unless you caught a bad band, then it was a bummer because
you had to wait out two songs. Most of the time it was good, though. There were
always two from Led Zeppelin, for instance.)

Just before I got home they started playing AC/DC. They played "For Those About to
Rock" and then they played "Back in Black."

That gave me an idea.

I went in the house and turned on the computer.
I searched "Back in Black drums" and several drum cover videos appeared.
I clicked on a couple but it was hard to see the drums the way they had shot the video.

Then I found "Five year old drums 'Back in Black'."
Ah, I thought, just my speed.
I watched that five year old play for a week; practiced doing what he did.
His dad was somewhere off camera, it seemed, playing guitar.

After a week and a half I started to get bored of the song or the kid, I couldn't tell which.
(The kid was always looking to his dad for approval.)
I noticed when the video ended another video to the side called "Six year old drums
'Welcome to the Jungle'."

I clicked on the video. Right away there was a world of difference between the five year old and the six year old. For one, I couldn't hear the six year old's father off camera. For another, the six year old was wearing sweat-shorts and he wasn't wearing a shirt and his hair was spiked with some sort of gel and he was smiling wildly at the camera.

You could tell this kid was going to be a real son of a bitch to women someday. Right away I decided I liked him. I decided I liked him a lot.

Wolfie

The only time I ever bought weed on a regular basis was what would have been my sophomore year in college.

I was on academic probation (i.e. not going to school), living in a large house with seven other people (plus my boyfriend and my roommate's boyfriend).

I took the bus three hours to my hometown once a month to buy weed from my mom's ex-husband, Steve, who everyone, including my mom, called 'Wolfie.'

(I called him Steve.)

They'd been divorced eight or nine years by then and I still sent him a Father's Day card every year along with my mom's other ex-husband, Stan, and my Uncle John and my grandfather.

(Having grown up without my biological father I was confused about what made someone a dad or parental figure in my life.)

I don't remember buying my biological father a Father's Day card.

It's hard to remember much about my biological father since he and my mom split up after the honeymoon.

Once I made pot brownies for everyone in the house but they weren't very good or we didn't get very high or something.

When I was an adolescent my mom would throw big parties at our house and make pot brownies and once I forgot and took a bite of one.

I spit it out on the kitchen floor and the dog ate it but I don't remember the dog acting funny or anything.

I didn't see Wolfie much after that year.

He moved in with a woman but he never had a child.

For a while he was living back with his parents, trying to detox from alcohol.

When I did see him after that he told me about having the DTs.

I kept sending him cards to various addresses.

I kept hearing hometown gossip about him getting better and then getting worse.

I took my daughter home after she was born so he could see her.

Then when she was eight he started calling me all the time.

(I think he got my number from his mom who I still saw with some frequency when I went 'home.')

At first I would answer when he called, but it was hard to understand him and I had a hard time getting off the phone.

I started letting his calls go to voicemail.

I'd wait a few days to listen to them.

They were always the same: drunken, mostly incoherent, ramblings, about him and my mom and me.

I didn't know what to do about the calls.

And they just kept coming.

Once I even got a call from his mother, which I also let go to voicemail.

(I called my mother, hoping she would know what to do but she didn't do anything either. She was remarried and living in Florida. She hadn't seen Steve in a long time either.)

Finally the calls stopped and I felt relieved.

I dealt with not knowing what to do by not doing anything.

(I had only thought of Steve in terms of being a father figure for me; I hadn't bothered to think of myself as a daughter for him or what that might mean or what my responsibility in that relationship might be.)

It was a year or so later that I got the newspaper clipping in the mail from his mom.

The clipping said he'd passed away from cancer but there'd been no mention of cancer before then.

I still didn't know what to do. I sent his mom and dad a card and avoided them whenever I went home after that.

I called my mom and my call went to voicemail.

I left a rambling, mostly incoherent message.

Jimmy

My daughter asked if we could stop by her friends' apartment on the way home.

She said she was buying weed from her friend's boyfriend for the river trip she was taking the next day.

I told her I still had weed at home in my drawer if she wanted some but she said my weed was weak, even though she'd never—to my knowledge—smoked it. "Jimmy's stuff is from the dispensary," she said.

"No offense," she said.

I wasn't offended. I was interested to meet Jimmy. I'd heard a lot about him.

When we walked inside the apartment there were four people sitting in chairs around a hookah: my daughter's two girlfriends, Jimmy and Jimmy's friend, Shank.

One of my daughter's friends asked if I wanted to see her bedroom and then both of my daughter's friends were on their feet and I was following them upstairs and looking at their bedrooms.

There were posters of Marilyn Monroe and James Dean.

There were covers of *The New Yorker*.

"Why do you have *New Yorker* covers?" I asked my daughter's friend.

"I found them," my daughter's friend said.

I hesitated, wanting to know more, but my daughter's other friend had called me into her room. There was a giant blanket on her wall made up of photographs of her with everyone she had ever known. I wasn't on it.

"Very nice," I said, not letting on my disappointment. "I like it a lot," I said.

We went back downstairs. I sat beside my daughter on the couch.

Shank tried to pass me a joint.

"No, thanks," I said. "My daughter doesn't want to smoke with me," I said.

"I have the opposite problem," Jimmy said.

"What do you mean?" my daughter said.

"I want my dad to smoke with me and he won't."

"I don't really want to smoke with her," I said.

I remembered smoking in a car with my mom and my boyfriend outside the bar where she worked when I was a senior in high school or a freshman in college.

It'd felt weird, like having sex with your brother or something.

Like it wasn't supposed to happen. Except there wasn't really any good feeling, either, just bad.

I remembered when I was eight and nine, sitting in the living room with my mom and my mom's husband and their friends. Someone would always accidentally pass me a joint.

And everyone would laugh.

I felt similarly now.

Everyone was laughing.

And now I'd met Jimmy.

Wolfie II

I never thought to ask why they called Steve 'Wolfie.'
I sent my mom a text to ask her.
After he died, she told me he'd been the love of her life.
I already knew that.
They were only married three or four years.
I was seven or eight when they married and we lived together in four different houses
    during that time.
One of the houses was 'out in the country' surrounded by Amish people.
There was an Amish school at the end of our road and an Amish store around the corner
    from that.
My mom sent me next door to buy eggs from our neighbors.
There were no children to play with because the Amish weren't allowed to play with non-
    Amish children and there weren't any other kind around.
My mom texted right back.
She said Steve had grown his hair and beard out 'for bicentennial days' and one of his
    friend's moms said he looked like a wolfman and it stuck.

I remember the night I realized my mom was having an affair.
A good friend of Steve's had moved in with us temporarily after his wife shot herself with
    his gun while he was at work.
"Big Ed." Big Ed wore overalls and had an even longer beard than Steve.
He was tall and sturdy like a lumberjack.
I remember sitting on his lap (I never sat on Steve's lap; Steve was only 5'5" or 5'6".), how
    low his voice was.
One night while Steve was at work, tending bar, the dog woke me, whining at the bottom of
    the stairs. I crept down in my nightgown, stood outside the door where Big Ed slept.
(It was the same room we played darts in.)
I remember feeling conflicted.
I remember trying to decide if I should go back up and get the tape recorder my
    grandfather had gotten me for Christmas.
Part of me wanted Steve to know what a horrible person my mother was.
But I couldn't do it; I knew my loyalty was to my mother.
I went back up to bed and the dog went with me.
I don't remember if it was days or weeks or months later that Steve moved out of the
    house and my mother and I moved into an apartment in town.
I remember I missed Big Ed, too.
I started sending Steve Father's Day cards soon after that.
I didn't send one to Big Ed.

Clue

We were playing Clue because it had rained so much the day before that my daughter's
boyfriend's softball game was cancelled.
Two of the guys from the team were playing with us.
They'd come over for pizza and beer before the game.
I was on a thirty day alcohol cleanse; I was Shaggy (it was the Scooby-Doo version of Clue).
"'Thirty day alcohol cleanse' makes it sound like you're cleansing yourself with alcohol,"
my daughter said. My daughter was Velma.
It was day seven and I wasn't drinking.
"Can I open a bottle of wine," my daughter said. My daughter was very responsible.
"Sure," I said. My daughter only ever had one glass, at least when I was around.
We took a break from the game so she could open the bottle.
I had to go to the bathroom; on my way back through the bedroom I stopped to check
my email.
It had been a week since I'd heard from the host of a reading series at which I was
supposed to be reading later in the summer. I'd sent her two emails to reconfirm
before buying a plane ticket.
I didn't like flying by myself but I had agreed to because she had been so complimentary.
"*Fast Machine* was one of my favorite books I read last year," she had said.
She had signed her emails with x's and o's. She had used a lot of exclamation points.
(That had been a couple months ago.)
Recently she had stopped replying to my emails.
I noticed one day her website had a listing for the reading and the next day it didn't.
I knew what was coming then. It was only a matter of waiting for it.
I'd been through a similar process several times in recent weeks.
The only thing of interest was how the person handled it, if they chose to tell the truth or
if they made up a story.
She made up a story.
She said she had to cancel the reading because of Comic-con.
I didn't mind. I felt only relief. And mild amusement.
I went back out into the dining room.
"Well, the reading's off. I don't have to fly anywhere now," I said.
"My mom's a 'rape apologist,' my daughter said, sarcastically, to the boys.
But the boys didn't know what we were talking about and didn't care.
The boys were still pissed about the game being cancelled; they wanted to vandalize the
field, tear down part of the fence.
I rolled a six, which put me in the dining room. (I didn't want to be in the dining room,
I wanted to be in the lounge, but the lounge was on the other side of the board and
there was only one die. It took forever to get anywhere.)
It took over an hour to solve the mystery. It turned out I, Shaggy, had done it in the
billiard room with the spell book.

(Shaggy seemed like an odd person to be carrying around a spell book, particularly in a billiard room, but I didn't question it, especially since I had made the accusation (i.e. won).)

Later I made a cup of licorice tea and went in the basement. It was still day seven of my alcohol cleanse.

But now I didn't have to fly anywhere. I didn't have to buy a ticket.

Taco Bell

It was a two hour drive,
An hour of highway and an hour of back roads that ran through small Ohio towns like the
      one I'd grown up in.
There were a lot of old cars in driveways, a lot of watery cornfields.
"Look, there's another tiny graveyard," my daughter said.
We had to fight the urge to stop and walk through every tiny graveyard.
"There's another pile of old cars," I said.
It was a similar urge and we fought this one similarly.

"Do you think Dad will want to go to lunch?" my daughter said.
"If he does, it'll be Taco Bell," I said.
"I could eat Taco Bell," my daughter said.
"Yeah," I said. "I'm down for Taco Bell."

I made a left onto the road that led into the park.
He was waiting on the porch, smoking a cigarette, when we pulled up.
My daughter sat on the couch and I sat in a rocking chair.
There were three cats but we only ever saw one.
My daughter's father brought us plates with slices of potato on them.
The three of us sat eating our potatoes, my daughter on the couch beside her father.

"I can't believe Mom forgot the time you almost shot her," my daughter said. It was one of
      her favorite family stories. It'd only recently come up. I couldn't remember how it'd
      come up.

"I guess I didn't think it was that big of a deal," I said.

"You didn't think a bullet practically grazing your head was a *big deal*?" my daughter said.

"I thought it was a bb gun or something," I said. "Besides, Paul was the one it grazed. I
      didn't feel a thing."

"I heard a noise in the closet," my daughter's father said. "I used the back end to move
      some clothes out of the way and the gun fired and the bullet went right between Paul
      and your mother."

"I sold my gun right after that," my daughter's father said.

"I would hope so," my daughter said, laughing.

After we finished our potatoes we went for a walk to the lake. The park where my
daughter's father lived was empty most of the year. People only came to stay in their
campers and trailers in the summer when it was warm and they could use the lake.
My daughter's father had moved down in late fall.

It was spring now and people were starting to trickle in.

"How do you like it down here?" one of us asked, my daughter or I.

"I hate it," he said. "They're way stricter with pot down here than in Michigan. They're
way more uptight about everything. It's a red state. They have me locked down, I
can't go anywhere without them tracking me. I want to buy a cheap car and drive to
Colorado."

I thought about the bag of pot I had in a drawer in the back of my closet, how I wasn't
smoking it, how it was just sitting there.

We were on the edge of the lake now. There were all these signs warning you about
swallowing the water. We stood and stared at it. Someone drove by on a golf cart. We
walked back to the trailer. I thought about how next time I'd bring some of the pot
with me.

"Do you want to hear the song I wrote for you?" my daughter's father said, meaning our
daughter. "I was going to get it made on a CD and get the lyrics printed for you and
everything before I moved but I never got the chance."

He was standing in front of the TV, holding a guitar.

There were Grateful Dead CDs on the floor next to a boom box. There were CDs and
cassette tapes both.

The song title was our daughter's name.

I can't remember the rest of the words.

Later, after he'd finished the song, he said he'd write them down for her.

We went outside on the porch and he started to roll a cigarette.

When he was finished rolling, we knew it was time to go.

"Do you still want to go to Taco Bell?" my daughter said as we pulled out onto the road.

"Sure," I said. "I could eat some Taco Bell."

But I was thinking about remembering to bring pot with me next time.

I was trying to remember the lyrics to the song about our daughter.

Wolfie III

I can only remember smoking weed with Steve once.

It was either right before or right after I married my daughter's father.

(We only knew each other a couple weeks before we got married though so it was
    probably after.)

I remember sitting on Steve's couch in a mobile home out by the lake.

Sixty Minutes was on so it must have been a Sunday.

Steve left to run an errand or to sell weed or something.

It seemed like he took forever.

But when he got back, *Sixty Minutes* was still on, so it couldn't have taken that long.

Snot Rockets

Tanja invited me to a craft show in Flint.
It was a Friday night and I didn't have anything else to do.
I'd never been to a craft show.

I'd been to a gun and knife show with my boyfriend, Evan, when I was nineteen.
Evan wasn't into guns but he had a collection of knives.
He also had a collection of skulls and a devil's lock and wore a spur on one combat boot
    and liked the band Gwar.
(That was about all I could remember about Evan.)

It turned out the Flint craft show wasn't in a big convention hall like the gun and knife
    show.
The Flint craft show was in a small café in downtown Flint called Lunch Café.
Tanja and Tanja's brother Willow and I carried in Tanja's 'zines and set them up on an
    indoor picnic table.
Next to us a woman was displaying crosses she claimed were bookmarks made from actual
    books. I wanted to ask her what books but she wasn't giving off a very friendly vibe.
Instead I stood next to Willow while he told me about a dream he'd had recently in which
    he had the words 'thug life' tattooed on his inner arm.
I looked and was surprised they weren't there already. I could have sworn they were
    already there.

The first hour of the craft show was slow.
The woman who ran the craft show kept coming up and saying, "wait until seven thirty,
    things really pick up around seven thirty."
It was only five fifteen.
Willow and I went for a walk to get food.
Someone had said there was a Mexican joint three blocks down.
We stopped at a corner, waited for the light.
There was a man waiting at the corner with us.
The man was in his late twenties and had a shaved head. I thought the man was attractive.
    We made eye contact. I may have smiled. (It's often hard for me to determine if I
    have smiled or not.)
Just before the light turned, the man bent over and blew a snot rocket onto the ground.
    Then the man started walking as though nothing had happened.

"Did you see that?" I said, when the man was out of earshot.
"See what?" Willow said.
"That man just blew a snot rocket right next to us."

"Oh yeah. Sometimes if your nose is running when you're out walking you have to clear it."

"On the sidewalk?" I said. I'd never had to clear my nose on the sidewalk.

"Yeah," Willow said.

"Girls don't clear their noses on sidewalks," I said.

Willow didn't say anything.

"What would you think if a girl blew her nose on the sidewalk?"

Willow didn't say anything.

"A young, pretty girl," I said.

Willow still didn't say anything.

"Would you be turned off?" I said.

"I'm thinking," Willow said.

Willow thought through our food ordering process and through our waiting for our food order and most of the walk back to the Lunch Café.

"I guess I'd think it was funny," Willow said, finally.

"You would?" I said.

"Yeah," Willow said. "I think I'd just laugh."

The three of us sat at the picnic table eating our burritos and nodding at people as they walked by.

A woman across from us was selling little tiny plastic cups of honey as a facial treatment. People seemed into the honey as facial treatment.

The woman next to us sold a bookmark.

A breastfeeding woman bought one of Tanja's 'zines.

I couldn't stop thinking about the snot rocket conversation I'd had with Willow.

I thought maybe I was being too uptight.

I tried picturing myself blowing a snot rocket on the street while a man watched.

For some reason I pictured myself sitting on the stoop of a 'brownstone,' bent over with my head between my knees when I did this.

I didn't know if this made it funnier or not.

I couldn't picture the man's reaction.

I'd never sat on the stoop of a brownstone.

I don't know why I pictured a brownstone.

At seven thirty it got busier, just like the host lady promised.

I didn't have any more time to think about snot rockets.

I had to think about selling 'zines. (It felt like it was 1992. I wanted to write 'slut' and 'whore' on my arms with a Sharpie but Tanja said she didn't have a Sharpie. I thought maybe she was just afraid of offending the host lady or the lady with the cross bookmarks.)

"Oh, I forgot," Willow said. "The tattoo had stuff going through the words."

"What stuff," I said, thinking, *please don't say barbed wire*.

"Like, snakes," Willow said.

"Oh," I said, not barbed wire. Maybe I was too uptight.

When the craft show was over we got in the front of Tanja's truck.

We passed the courthouse where my husband and I had signed our divorce papers.

We passed the hospital where my daughter was born.

We passed the library where I'd gone to see Robert Pinsky read.

Willow was begging Tanja to stop at a hookah lounge.

I couldn't stop thinking of the image of me sitting on a brownstone stoop, blowing a snot rocket between my knees.

I liked this image of me better.

We stopped for a light. A man stood on the corner beside a woman. The man smiled, he had no top teeth. He looked about fifty or sixty. He bent over the woman beside him. The woman was wearing sweatpants and an oversized Garfield sweatshirt. The woman was ten, fifteen years younger. I could imagine the woman blowing a snot rocket on the sidewalk. He kissed her on the top of her head.

I liked this image a lot.

Evan

That's not true. I remember a lot more.
I remember a lot of things.

Brutus

Tanja and I were in a bar in my hometown in Ohio.

It was the bar I had grown up in.

My childhood friend and her husband were there too.

There was a picture of Brutus, the Ohio State University mascot on the wall.

Tanja was from California. Tanja pointed to it and said, "What's that? a potato?"

My childhood friend's husband looked like he was going to pass out.

"No," I said. "It's not a potato."

"A loaf of bread?" Tanja said.

"No," I said. "It's not a loaf of bread."

This was a fun game we were playing. I didn't want to stop playing the fun game with Tanja.

Punk House

The Sunday after the craft show in Flint, Tanja said there was a craft show in Detroit.

I was interested to see what a craft show in Detroit would look like (now that I had
     something to compare it to).

Tanja said the craft show was from noon to five.

It was an hour drive; it was already one; I couldn't make a decision.

I texted Tanja, "What's it like there?"

"It's a punk house," Tanja texted back.

I didn't know what a punk house was.

I pictured a lot of angry young men with high testosterone and angry young women
     wearing leather and lip piercings.

It was pouring rain and the streets were flooded and I almost turned around before I even
     got to the highway.

I decided to keep going because I liked listening to music alone in the car.

(It was the same reason I liked mowing the lawn and going for walks at eleven pm.)

I was wearing black cutoffs and a black bil-a-bong tank top.

I didn't feel very punk but I didn't feel very anything else either.

I parked outside the house and walked inside.

I couldn't hear or see anyone. Then I heard a man upstairs flush a toilet and cough.

I thought I had the wrong address.

I went back to my car to text Tanja.

Tanja met me on the sidewalk.

The craft show was in a garage-like enclosure around the side of the house.

Tanja was sharing a table with a young woman who made patches. The woman had
     rainbow colored hair that was shaved on one side but she didn't seem particularly
     angry. She was holding hands with a man in some sort of jeanie pant. The man's hair
     was in a bun. He didn't seem angry either.

"She tells everyone they're made from stolen materials," Tanja said. "That's her selling
     point."

"I'm going to steal one," I said.

The woman with rainbow hair and the man in jeanie pants were discussing religion with
     a nondescript man I can't describe. The man in jeanie pants was saying something
     negative about Goodwill and Volunteers of America. (At least one of them was
     affiliated with a religion!)

He said, "I used to be open to religion, to everyone believing what they want, but now
     I'm, like, no, no way."

I guess that was his idea of anger.

The woman with rainbow hair said, "Yeah, why do I need some ghost man in the sky to love me when I can love myself."

I stopped listening. I felt duped by Tanja. Maybe I was too old. Maybe it was a generational thing. I couldn't imagine any punk I'd ever heard of or met talking about loving themselves.

I looked around the room. Everyone looked the same to me: similarly sized arm tattoos, tights with shorts, consciously minimal makeup, pale skin, brown hair, nondescrip bodies.

People went outside to smoke. I didn't understand why people went outside to smoke.

The table next to me was filled with pamphlets. I reached over and picked one up. It was very long and about living off the grid. I couldn't image anyone present living off the grid.

I didn't understand why anyone was charging money for anything; why Tanja had to pay ten dollars for her table.

Everyone was very polite. I didn't understand why everyone was so polite. (No one talked to me.)

"Maybe it's a misuse of the word 'punk'," Tanja said, when I brought up my questions/ grievances. "Maybe they need a different word."

I guessed my expectations had been too high.
These just seemed like regular hipsters to me.
(Radiohead was playing on a boombox across from us.)
Hipsters with a faux hippie attitude.
Maybe I was being too harsh. (Maybe I was just angry.)

I didn't think anyone here would blow snot rockets on the sidewalk.

But Tanja sold a lot of 'zines. The punks loved Tanja's 'zines.

Third Eye Blind

We were still in the bar I'd grown up in in my hometown.
Earlier we'd been at the Elk's lounge drinking dollar beers.
(We weren't members but someone—a drunk patron—had waved us in from the patio
    where he was smoking and the bartender had allowed us to stay.)
We'd gone to the bowling alley bar first but the bowling alley bar was closed now. You
    could get drinks from the main counter but it wasn't the same as sitting at the bar.

Next to the Elk's lounge were a Laundromat and a karate studio.
It looked like a scene from *Fight Club* inside the karate studio.
There were fifteen to twenty men on the mats; they kept changing which man they
    singled out to circle/tag team.
We stood outside the window watching for a long time.
A woman wearing a pro-life shirt kept turning around and looking at us.
There were about forty other people watching with her, mostly women and children.
Eventually the pro-life woman came outside and stood next to us.
"They're going for their black belts. Don't worry. This is normal," she said.
We nodded and she went back inside. I wondered which man was hers.
And if he was getting his black belt.

At the bar I'd grown up in a man with a tattoo on his forearm that said Southpaw was
    talking to us.
I'd overheard a woman greeting him asking about his probation being recently lifted.
The man kept saying, "are you making fun of me?" to Tanja and me because we kept
    laughing.
I wondered if he had a black belt. (We weren't making fun of him. We were just having a
    good time.)
The man was extremely intoxicated. He kept leaning over our table. His cigarette
    dangerously close to our heads. He reminded me of every guy I had gone to high
    school with.
There was a high suicide rate in my hometown; a high rate of overdoses also.

Later we were trying to leave.
It was late and we still had to go to my friend's house on the other side of town.
(My friend was reclusive. You couldn't get her to leave her house to go to a bar anymore.
    You had to take a bottle of wine to her.)
The southpaw guy didn't want us to go.
His leaning had increased to the point of . . .
He was telling us about his exwife, his kids.
We were making our gentle goodbyes, Tanja and me.
We stood up from the picnic table.

The southpaw guy's eyes were . . .
We took a step away, looked back.
NEVER LOOK BACK!
A new song came on the jukebox.
It was the one I always confuse with another song by Oasis.
I wish you would step back from that ledge, my friend
The entire bar erupted in song.
Or, the girls throwing darts started singing.
Tanja and I started singing also.

"Okay," we said.
"One more song," we said.

Big Mistake

Today I found myself quoting the famous scene from *Pretty Woman* aloud in the car as though addressing a person who wasn't there. Last week I heard myself recite the same lines while addressing myself. It's hard to say which felt more applicable.

You Alone Decide What's Real

Tanja and I were competing to see who had moved the most as a child.

"I know of at least fourteen places we lived before I was eighteen," I said.

Tanja started naming places she had lived. She kept naming her grandma's house over and over, between every place.

"You can't count your grandma's house more than once," I said, even though I wasn't sure if this was fair or not.

"Okay, " Tanja said.

Not counting her grandma's place more than once, Tanja named fourteen houses and apartments. Same as me. Tied!

Then I received a new text from my mom listing four more apartments we had lived in before the first place I could remember living.

"That makes eighteen places for me," I said. "Eighteen different houses and apartments in eighteen years."

I think if I had allowed Tanja to count all the times they had moved back in with her grandma, she would have easily beat me.

But I didn't allow this.

And so I won. (I was the most fucked up!)

I thought about texting everyone in my contact list to tell them this. I would tell them this and then I would say, "Does *that* explain anything? LOL." But then I remembered half the people in my contact list didn't ever want to hear from me again.

I wondered how many people didn't want to ever hear from Tanja.

I didn't think it would be as many. I thought I would win that competition too. (I'm still the most fucked up!)

I thought about deleting the people who never wanted to hear from me again from my contact list but I couldn't remember who those people were or I had a hard time saying goodbye or both.

Alt-Rock

On the drive home from Ohio we listened to Tanja's Pandora station.
Tanja liked 90's Alternative rock. (I liked it, too, but it was more surprising that Tanja did.)

She had a theory about each song we listened to.
For instance, she claimed the song 'Closing Time' was about a baby being born.
I listened to the lyrics.
The lyrics were clearly about finding a girl in a bar at the end of the night.
"That's just the surface meaning," Tanja said. "You have to listen to the deeper meaning,"
    she said.
I listened as deep as I could.
I didn't hear anything about a baby being born.
I thought maybe Tanja was crazy. Or pulling my leg.

Tanja said the song 'The Freshman' by the Verve Pipe was about a girl dying at a party.
    She said the guy in the Verve Pipe had heard the story from someone else. He wrote
    another song about how he felt bad writing about someone else's story.

Tanja said something about the band Eve 6 but I don't remember what she said.
I remember telling Tanja that Eve 6 sounded like the name of a girls' R&B group from the
    '90s, like SWV, not an alternative band.
Tanja disagreed.
Tanja seemed to feel strongly about Eve 6 so I let it go.

Tanja seemed to feel strongly about the band Tonic also but in a different way.
(I had never even heard of Tonic, though I recognized the song.)
Tanja had a problem with their song, 'If You Could Only See.'
(I'd never given the song much thought; had barely listened to the lyrics.)

"I just think the guy seems delusional; thinking this woman's eyes actually change color,
    to a deeper shade of blue, when he's around, or whatever...He just sounds obsessed.
    I imagine his friends are like, 'dude, her eyes don't change color. She doesn't actually
    love you.'"

"But that's why he's saying that," I said. "That's why he's like, 'if you could only see,'
    because he knows his friends don't believe him but he wants them to see."

Tanja made a face. Tanja had a problem with that song that wasn't going to be cleared up
    in a five minute conversation in the car.

The one band/song I wanted Tanja to have a theory about, she didn't.

Tanja didn't have anything to say about Silverchair's 'Tomorrow.'

I couldn't get over the lyrics.

I wanted to know why the water was so hard to drink or what that was a metaphor for.

"Maybe it's not a metaphor for anything," Tanja said. "Maybe the water in Australia or wherever they're from is literally hard to drink."

I felt unsatisfied with this answer.

I couldn't believe a person who thought 'Closing Time' was about the birth of a baby, didn't have a theory about 'Tomorrow.'

I felt duped by Tanja. I was beginning always to feel duped now by Tanja.

I didn't understand why 'Cumbersome' never came on Tanja's Pandora station. I kept waiting for 'Hey Man, Nice Shot' to come on also.

I felt a little duped.

Suicide

We were on a rooftop in Brighton, MI.
(You've never heard of Brighton unless you're from MI.)
We'd just been told the restaurant didn't serve tacos on the rooftop.
Nowhere on a sign or on the menu did it say this.
But this is what the waitress said—"You can't get tacos on the rooftop."—
when Willow asked.
So no one got tacos. We didn't want to sit inside.

We'd spent the day doing Internet searches and making calls to local wildlife centers.
Tanja and Willow had found three baby bats in the basement of their house the day
    before.
Tanja had tried feeding them some sort of mixture of water and salt and sugar she'd read
    about online.
(They'd actually found six baby bats in total but one was badly decomposed when they
    found it and one had died recently and the third had disappeared from the box Tanja
    left them in on the porch overnight.)
Our Internet searches and calls had led us to a woman in Brighton.
The woman had pulled each baby bat from the bag and held it without gloves, spread
    open its tiny wings.
It'd been hard to leave them.
(The smallest had a broken wing, the woman showed us. It was hardest to leave this one.)

There was a three pound burger on the menu
It was a sort of challenge: your picture on the wall, a t-shirt.
Willow was considering it.
"It says you have to eat it in thirty minutes," Tanja said.
"I think I can do it," Willow said.
"I want to see you do it, but not when I have to drive you home," I said.
"They don't even give it to you free if you do it," Tanja said.
It seemed like you should at least get the burger free if you ate it all in thirty minutes.

"I wonder how the bats are doing," Tanja said.
"I want to apprentice with her," I said. "Learn everything about bats."
"Me, too," Tanja said.
In attempting to make the baby bats comfortable, we'd watched videos of how to care for
    them online.
In every video someone had swathed a baby bat in a blanket, stuck a small binky in
    its mouth.

We didn't know where to get the small binky.

We didn't think the woman would want to apprentice us.

Our burgers came. They were normal sized.

Country music was playing. I recognized all the songs.

"Country music is the saddest music there is," Willow said.

"Where did you hear that," I said. "Country music makes me happiest."

Tanja didn't have an opinion. Or if she had one she didn't state it.

"More people commit suicide listening to country music than any other music,"
     Willow said.

"I don't think that's true," I said.

"Where'd you hear that," Tanja said.

Willow couldn't cite where he'd heard that.

On the car drive home we were still talking about suicide.

Someone Willow knew back in California had just killed himself.

Someone Tanja knew, too.

Two different people, I mean, from the same town.

"More people die of suicide in this country than breast cancer," I said.

"Really?" Tanja said.

"Also car related fatalities," I said.

Tanja told us a story she'd heard that week about a teenage girl who'd jumped off a
     highway overpass after her father had publicly shamed her in a Youtube video.

"There's an increase in the rise of suicides among men in their fifties and sixties," I said.

"I can't imagine ever being at that point," Tanja said. "Where I thought the next day
     wouldn't be better."

I didn't say anything. Maybe I'd been close to that point. I couldn't imagine jumping off
     an overpass but I could imagine sitting in my car in the garage. I could imagine
     turning on a gas stove.

I felt somewhat duped by Tanja. It seemed impossible she'd never thought about suicide.
     It was hard for me to understand a person being alive, having not considered suicide.

I thought maybe if I could apprentice with the bat woman I would feel differently. I
     thought about all the tiny bats in the videos, swaddled next to each other, sucking on
     their binkies.

The woman had said the bat with the broken wing probably wouldn't make it. It was so
     hard to leave it.

Jim Carrey

I was watching the Jerry Seinfeld Internet show—
'Funny people drinking caffeinated drinks,' or whatever it's called.
I watched the Amy Schumer episode and she seemed nervous but still managed to say the
    word 'vagina' three times and then I saw that the most recent video was available
    and that it was Jim Carrey.
Right away Jim Carrey seemed manic in a way that reminded me of Robin Williams.
I felt uncomfortable right away (is what I'm saying).
I didn't feel any better as the show progressed.
Everything Jim did screamed 'I am going to be the next celebrity to kill myself/I am not
    okay'
He talked about being on a twenty-one day cleanse and leaving for some retreat where he
    wouldn't be speaking for five days.
He didn't eat at the diner with Jerry or drink coffee like the other guests.
He drank hot water or tea and stood on his seat to drop the artificial sweetener he had
    brought with him into his cup.
Later he took Jerry to his art studio and there were seemingly a thousand tubes of paint.
All I could think of was that creepy video he made for Emma Stone a couple years back,
    the one in which he 'jokingly' asked her out but everyone—including Emma—knew
    he wasn't *really* joking.
I felt like I could relate to Jim Carrey in that moment.
Maybe I just felt uncomfortable watching the episode because I didn't want to relate to
    Jim Carrey.

After it ended I clicked on the Jimmy Fallon episode in the same way you watch a funny
    TV show or movie after watching a horror movie as a kid: so you can go to sleep.

Jimmy was kind of boring but at least I didn't relate to him.

Things I Don't Tell My Daughter

I break down sobbing at random moments now.//Today was the first day I felt comfortable enough on the drums to 'just jam.'//I am probably not going to be okay.// Sometimes I listen to the same song on repeat for an hour and a half in the basement so I can go to sleep.//There is no alcohol in the house anymore because I don't trust myself around alcohol anymore.//Sometimes I put my laptop under her bed before she gets home at night and take it out after she has left for work the next day.//I am not as strong as she thinks (but I am probably stronger than *this*).

Rad Pessimist

I was visiting an old friend at her parents' house.

I had brought with me an iced coffee.

It was summer and humid and I wasn't drinking alcohol.

When I finished the iced coffee I rinsed the plastic cup in the sink.

I couldn't remember where the garbage can was located.

I asked my friend for help locating the garbage can.

She pointed to a location beside the fridge and I walked over.

I used my foot to open the lid like I'd seen people do on TV and in the movies.

I was about to drop the plastic cup into the garbage can when my friend took it from
my hand.

"They'll want to recycle that," she said, meaning her parents.

She took the plastic cup somewhere I couldn't see and when she returned we didn't
discuss it further.

"Who wants to play Go Fish," my friend said. And I said I did. Because I'd brought the
deck of cards that said 'Go Fish' on the outside.

My friend and I sat cross-legged on the floor and oh yeah my friend has two daughters
who sat on the floor with us.

We're not psychopaths.

We were playing Go Fish with two small girls.

On the drive home I had time to think about the plastic cup.

I imagined a scenario in which I asked for it back.

"Just, you know, I brought it here and I thought I'd take it with me," I imagined myself
saying.

"You don't want my parents to recycle it?" I imagined my friend asking.

I imagined my friend's parents, who would be home from their golf game by now, looking
up over the tops of their newspaper at me.

Maybe I was a psychopath, was what they were intimating.

"I don't know," I would say. "I just . . . I thought I'd make that decision later—to recycle or
not—at home, after I've thought about it a while."

I wouldn't mention feeling offended earlier when my original choice had been overturned.

When I got home I told my daughter about the plastic cup and the scenario I'd imagined
on the drive home.

"Why are you such a psychopath," my daughter said.

"Who doesn't want to recycle a plastic cup," she said.

"It's not that I didn't want to recycle . . . " I started to say.

"I'm going upstairs," my daughter said.

Kenny Chesney

My daughter and I were arguing over which one of us walked on eggshells more around
the other.

It was hard to determine who was winning because it was hard to determine if the winner
was the one who walked on eggshells more or the one who walked on eggshells less.

"Anyway," my daughter said. "I'm not interested in walking on eggshells. That's not my
personality."

I couldn't tell if she'd won or not.

"I'm going upstairs," she said.

It felt like she'd won.

Gerald

Today (like, five minutes ago) I was masturbating on my bed with a hairbrush and thinking about volunteering later today at the therapeutic equestrian center where I volunteer on Mondays and sometimes Tuesdays. I was thinking about writing this story I have wanted to write for a while now, which is a story about Gerald, a rider at the therapeutic equestrian center where I volunteer. Gerald is nineteen or twenty or maybe he is twenty-one now, I'm not sure. Gerald has Down syndrome and you aren't supposed to 'talk down to' or 'baby talk' him or anyone else who rides but inevitably people do. Gerald's mother also volunteers at the therapeutic equestrian center and one day I was walking on one side of a horse while she was walking on the other and she was telling us (the horse leader and me) about a day recently in which she discovered Gerald had created a Facebook account for himself. "There were quite a few *less than desirable* people he had friended on there," she said. "I defriended them and explained to Gerald . . . and now I keep an eye on his account." I wondered what she meant by 'less than desirable people." I thought she could mean someone like *me*. Or me, even. (But very quickly I remembered I'm not on Facebook so I guess it wasn't me.) Later, during one of our break periods between riders, I was sitting with Gerald and a couple other volunteers. Gerald's mother wasn't in the break room with us. She was in the barn putting away a horse or talking to another horse leader. Gerald was drinking a juice box and one of the other volunteers, a young woman in high school, said, "Gerald, what flavor is your juice box?" and Gerald said, "Apple!" and the young woman in high school said, "That sounds yummy," and Gerald said, "Yes, it's very yummy," in a way that sort of ran all of the syllables of all of the words together in one robotic sound. I thought about how we had been told not to talk down to or baby talk the riders but I didn't say anything. I never said anything in the break room (or to Gerald) other than "hey" or "it sure is hot/cold/raining." Another volunteer, a middle aged woman with hip problems, came in from outside and said, "Hey, there's a double rainbow!" and we all got up from the plastic chairs and went to the windows to look at the double rainbow. Gerald came too. Someone had called Gerald over. The young woman in high school, maybe. We all stepped back and encouraged Gerald to look out the window. "See the double rainbow?" we said. "Yeah!" Gerald said. One of us traced an outline for each rainbow on the window in front of Gerald to make sure he saw. Then we sat back down in the plastic chairs. One of us went outside to get a better picture of the double rainbow on our phone. Gerald's mother came into the break room from the back. She said, "So-and-so said there's a double rainbow. Gerald, did you see the double rainbow?" "Yeah!" Gerald said. Then the rest of us echoed him. "Yeah," we said. "We showed Gerald the double rainbow." But Gerald's mother seemed like she wasn't listening. Or Gerald's mother wanted to show Gerald herself. She held open the door for Gerald. "Come on out and see the double rainbow, Gerald," she said. We watched as she took Gerald outside and traced the rainbows in front of Gerald as we had already done five minutes earlier. "You see them?" she said. "Yeah!" Gerald said. I watched, wondering again about the 'less than desirable people' Gerald had followed on Facebook. I imagined the less than desirable people were female porn stars. I wondered if Gerald had ever watched a porn or masturbated. I wondered if "not talking down to' or 'talking baby talk' to Gerald included allowing him to be a pervert like the rest of us. I thought of all this with the hairbrush inside me. Now I am typing this up. In a few minutes I will take a bath so I don't smell like my sex before I go to the therapeutic equestrian facility where I will see Gerald. I will say, "Hey!"

Maker's Mark Mint Julep

I hadn't had any alcohol to drink in forty-two days.
I had told myself I wouldn't drink for thirty but once you stop doing something it's hard
    to start doing it again.
A week earlier I had told my friends I would drink wine with them.
Then when the time came to drink wine I couldn't bring myself to drink it.
I kept filling their glasses hoping they wouldn't notice.
I made myself a cup of licorice tea after they left and drank it by myself in the basement.
I was procrastinating my return to drinking a while longer.
I couldn't tell if I feared alcohol or myself and it didn't seem to matter which.

Yesterday I found a bottle of Maker's Mark Mint Julep on the top shelf of a bookcase in
    the basement (it was Day Forty-Two).
Instead of red wax it had green.
It had been there on the top shelf a long time.
I had to rinse the dust off of it before I opened it.
I filled a glass with ice and poured some in.
It tasted sweet and the sweetness helped to ease my fears.

I was watching *Henry and June* in the basement.
I had seen the movie before but not in a long time.
In the movie Henry Miller's wife June is unhappy with the way Henry has portrayed her
    on the page.

"You make everything ugly!" the movie-version June says.

This was the reason I didn't want to write about myself anymore
I was afraid of making myself—and everyone around me—ugly.

But I couldn't seem to stop myself.
I wondered if Henry had ever tried to stop himself as I poured myself another glass of
    Mint Julep.
I wondered if Henry ever tried to stop as I wrote another poem about myself.

Mickey and Mallory Are My Spirit Animals

I was in a casino in California.
You weren't allowed to use dice in a casino in California.
But I was playing slots (so that didn't apply to me).
The slot machine I was playing featured white tigers.
I didn't care about white tigers.
I'd picked the machine for the absence of people on the neighboring machines.
(I didn't like people.)
I put in twenty dollars.
The most I had ever won playing twenty dollars was sixty dollars.
I played for ten minutes.
I was up to forty dollars.
I thought I might top my highest win.
A cocktail waitress came around and I waved her away.
I didn't drink in casinos.
(I only drank alone in my basement!)
I was up to fifty-five.
Two men sat down next to me.
I caught myself catch my breath.
Outwardly I pulled a lever.
Inwardly I made this sound: fuuuuuuuuuuuck.
One of the men put money in one of the machines
(fuuuuuuuuuck).
I couldn't see what he looked like.
It didn't matter.
I pulled a lever and lost five dollars.
I pulled the lever again and lost five more.
"How do you play these?" one of the men said to me
(fuuuuuuuuuuuck).
it didn't matter which one.
"I don't know," I said, staring straight ahead at my machine.
I increased my bet and pulled the lever.
"What's your name?" one of the men said.
I stared ahead.
It didn't matter which one.
"I don't speak," I said.
I increased my betting.
I was down to nine dollars.
I was down to six dollars.

I increased my bet.
I waited to bottom out.
I couldn't wait to bottom out.

Eternal Sunshine Faggot

I was watching *Eternal Sunshine of the Spotless Mind*. I had only planned to watch the first fifteen minutes but after fifteen minutes I couldn't stop watching. At one point, after the fight that leads to their break up, Jim Carrey is driving in a car and Kate Winslet is walking on the sidewalk trying to get away from him, and Kate Winslet yells, "Get out of my face, faggot!" I had been smoking a cigarette when Kate Winslet yelled this and I sort of reverse-inhaled the smoke and coughed it back out several times. It'd been eleven years since I'd seen the film in the theater. A lot had happened in the culture since then. Social media had happened, I mean. I got out my computer. I looked on Twitter to see if there was any outrage already in place to which I could add my name. I did a Google search of Charlie Kaufman's name to see if his star on the walk of fame had been revoked. I couldn't find anything right off the bat but I kept looking!

Joe C. (RIP)

I wish there was a way to laugh at the beginning or end of a poem like rappers do at the beginnings of songs or like Kid Rock does at the end of 'Bawitdaba.' One time a guy I liked told me a story about a girl he had liked in the past. He said, "I liked her a lot until she told me her favorite song was 'Bawitadba.' After that I knew it was never going to happen between us." I felt similarly about the guy I liked after he told me that story. I knew it was never going to happen between us now that he'd told me he didn't like a girl because her favorite song was 'Bawitada.' HAHAHAHAHAHAHA!

Real Artist

I was talking to a new friend at a gathering at my house.
I don't remember what I was saying.
My new friend interrupted me to say, "You seem like you live like a real artist."
My new friend had already been twice published by *The New Yorker*.
I thought maybe she had confused me with herself.
I had a collection of stories that wasn't even carried in most bookstores.
"What?" I said.
"I feel like all I do is run errands," my new friend said.

I didn't know what my new friend thought constituted living 'like a real artist' or what I
    had said or done to make her think I did.
(My new friend worked in academia and I rarely left the house.)
Maybe she had confused a lack of ambition, goals and work ethic with being a real artist.
Maybe I had been speaking about my life in a whiny or pretentious manner
(as I am probably doing now in these poems)
and she had confused my lamentations with living like a real artist.

Maybe she was calling me bohemian or temperamental or phony.

The more I thought about it, the more I began to think my new friend had knowingly or
    unknowingly insulted me.
Or maybe I had knowingly or unknowingly insulted myself.

(My new friend was recently offered a job at a more prestigious university and it is likely I
    will not see her again.)

I began to write a poem about my new friend.
She had a novel coming out with a big press.
And I was living like a real artist, writing poems for free in my bedroom.

Two Days Ago

It was eight thirty or nine. I didn't think my daughter would be home until eleven or twelve. Earlier in the day I had been unable to stop crying, then I had managed to stop, and now I couldn't stop crying again. I was sort of hyperventilating and blowing my nose a lot. It was the worst it'd been in weeks and I attributed it to the weather because I didn't know what else to attribute it to or I was uncomfortable attributing it to anything else. I was on the stepstool in the kitchen when I heard the garage door open. Earlier in the summer I had hidden mini bottles of wine and champagne in a cabinet over the refrigerator. Now I wanted the bottles back but when I heard the garage door open my immediate instinct was to leave the bottles where they were and to come down off the stepladder and to pretend like I hadn't been crying. I tried to stand far from my daughter with my back to her but when she didn't immediately go upstairs I had to walk toward her. I stood closer to her, wondering if she could tell I had spent the last hour crying. I didn't think it was possible for her not to tell. I knew my face was red and my eyes were swollen and my voice when I talked sounded scratchy. I kept sniffling so that my nose wouldn't run. I said, "I was just about to go for a walk," which was the truth, hoping she wouldn't want to go with me. "If you wait fifteen minutes I'll go with you," she said. "You don't have to," I said. "No, I want to," she said. I went in my bathroom and splashed cold water on my face and blew my nose. It was already dark by the time we walked which was good because it meant she couldn't look at me. We began to talk, but something about the conversation felt surreal or like we were in a movie or something. I felt subdued or slightly drugged or something. I avoided eye contact and neither of us brought up my crying or the reason why I had been crying and after she went upstairs to watch TV on her phone and I went into the basement to listen to music and to drink the wine I'd gotten back out of the cabinet after she'd gone upstairs.

Panic in Needle Park

We were walking through Times Square on the hottest day of the year in New York City.
I was way closer than I wanted to be to tens of thousands of people who probably didn't
    want to be close to me either.
I had the thought that I missed the days when Times Square was filled with junkies and
        prostitutes then felt full of shit because I'd only known that Times Square from
        watching '70s movies and reading books (and because I would probably hate junkies
        and prostitutes if I encountered them outside of movies and books).
My daughter said, "How long is this show going to last?"
"I don't know," I said.
I was beginning to question why I had purchased tickets for a show neither of us seemed
    to want to see.

(I knew it had something to do with wanting to expose my daughter to things to which I
        had not been exposed which had something to do with always putting my daughter
        first which had to do with proving I was a 'better' parent than my mother which was
        super fucked up and hypocritical and judgmental and also, according to a therapist
        I saw four or five times in 2010, a main reason for the failure of my romantic
        relationships.)

Fifteen minutes later we were finally inside the theater.
I handed our tickets to the ticket taker who scanned them and then informed me they
    were for the wrong night.
"Take them to the box office, maybe they can help you," the man said.
But at the box office we were told there was nothing they could do; the tickets were for the
    previous Saturday night, and tonight they were sold out.
We walked back out into Times Square.
My daughter didn't say anything; maybe she was waiting for me to sulk.
We turned right off of the main road and onto a quieter side street.
I pulled a small bottle of Jack Daniel's from my purse, opened it and took a drink.
"What are you doing?" my daughter said.
(It was uncharacteristic of me to carry bottles of alcohol in my purse or to drink outside of
    my basement.)
"I was going to surprise you with it later," I said.
I handed the bottle out to her.
She made a face and shook her head.
"We can't drink on the street like crackheads," she said.
I pulled her into an alcove of a store front, took another drink and handed her the
    bottle again.
"We're in New York City. No one gives a shit," I said.

I couldn't remember ever drinking like this with my mother.

I was always 'too good' to drink with my mother; always too busy proving something to her or to myself; it was hard to judge someone if you joined them, I guess, was the point of my abstinence.

"We don't have any chaser," my daughter said.

She hadn't yet learned to like the taste of alcohol, only the effects.

"I have a bottle of water," I said.

My daughter took a drink from the bottle, made a scrunched up face, and then laughed.

It was going to be a different sort of night than the one we had planned.

We walked down the street, taking swigs in random alcoves.

A few blocks down we walked by a large glass storefront with hockey jerseys hanging in the windows.

It was muggy, even at eight thirty in the evening, and the store, we reasoned, would probably have good air conditioning.

We went inside and regretted that no one we knew was into hockey.

The a/c was blasting and we stood and watched a fight break out in an old hockey game they were showing on a big screen in the back of the store.

Back on the street outside a teenage girl was sitting on the sidewalk alone, smoking a cigarette and taking a photograph of herself with a selfie stick.

The next day we would see *Fun Home* and go to the Museum of Natural History and the day after that we would walk by the Chelsea Hotel and the Stonewall Inn and eat lunch near Washington Square Park but I was no better than my mother.

I was a fake and a phony and I don't want this awareness to come off as maturity (or as any sort of admirable quality) on my part because it's not.

My mother was always her authentic self and I was living a life I didn't necessarily want to live (because I wanted people to like me or because I wanted to be perceived as 'good').

In the airport three days later my daughter got a series of texts from my mom.

"She wants me to be her partner in her football pool this year," my daughter said.

(My daughter was in a fantasy football league with her friends; I had texted my mother a picture of her reading a fantasy football magazine on the flight to New York City.)

I didn't know anything about football.

"Cool," I said.

They had struggled with a relationship for years and I had conveniently blamed that on my mother but I realized now I had done nothing to foster or encourage a relationship between them either.

"That will be good for you guys, to have something to talk about each week," I said.

"Yeah," my daughter said.

I didn't know how to tell my daughter everything so I told her some things and kept everything else hidden. Sort of like the dad in *Fun Home*. I was sort of like the dad in *Fun Home*, I mean. My mother was nothing like the dad in *Fun Home*. My mother had nothing to hide.

JOA

Joa said his name was Joa but he didn't look like a Joa and I didn't believe him.

He was sitting on a stool in a kitchen and six of us were standing in a semi circle around him.

He looked like the lead singer of Pearl Jam when the lead singer of Pearl Jam sang about a boy named Jeremy.

I decided Joa's real name was Jeremy (or Joe or Joel).

(Later I found out it was Joel.)

Joa wanted my stepdaughter to live on a commune with him on the border of Idaho in northeastern Washington.

(This was why Joa was here; they'd met on Craigslist and now he was here to 'interview' her in person.)

Secretly I hated Joa.

Joa had an iPhone on which he kept track of his steps and said shit like, "I stay away from GMOs to keep my alkaline levels in place" and "Today I already had ten thousand steps by two p.m.!"

Joa told a long story about a guy named Esu who had saved his life or transformed his life or in some way brainwashed him and started the commune (I decided Esu's real name was Eddie).

"Esu told me that if a friend doesn't want to let you go, that friend is not being a good friend. A friend shouldn't try to guilt you into maintaining a friendship," Joa said.

I didn't understand other ways of maintaining friendships other than guilt.

Guilt was my main motivation for living in general.

Joa made contradictory statements like "we live totally off the grid" and "I'm never going to have a job again" and "once a month we make a run to Costco" and "I told the cop that was cool cuz I didn't need a license anymore anyway."

I thought Joa was full of shit (and wondered how he had driven over without a license and who paid the insurance on his car and stuff like that).

But my stepdaughter seemed to like him so I couldn't say this.

I leaned against the counter thinking how full of shit Joa was with my arms crossed instead.

At the end of Joa's speech he insisted on hugging everyone in the room.

"Most people hug on the right side," Joa said, before he hugged the first person.

"But the heart is on the left side. You should always hug heart to heart," Joa said, making a bigger production of hugging than I thought the situation warranted.

I stood as far from Joa as I could manage with my arms folded in front of my heart.
I waited for Joa to approach me.
I had not decided if I would refuse a hug or not.
Then Joa did something unexpected.
He hesitated a second in front of me and kept walking toward the next person.
I was the only person who hadn't had to hug Joa and I felt a sense of accomplishment about that.

Later I sat with my stepdaughter after her date with Joa.
She told me they'd spent most of the five hours they were together picking up bicycles from one location and delivering them to another
while Joa ate convenience store nachos and smoked electronic cigarettes.

I wanted to point out several of Joa's contradictory statements to my stepdaughter.
But then she said something that made me change my mind.
She said, "But I really like him."
And suddenly I remembered liking guys like Joa when I was twenty-two also.
I was pretty sure I would have liked Joa.
I was pretty sure I would have wanted Joa to hug me heart to heart.

Everyone Hates Me Now, So What?

We were discussing pressure a female friend of ours was feeling to get married.

"Why wouldn't she want to marry—," my daughter said.

"I don't know," I said. I listed three or four practical possibilities: timing - the antiquity of the institution—the disallowance of people from different age groups to marry—a lifelong avoidance of true intimacy and commitment . . .

Then I said, "Or maybe she just doesn't want to feel like a possession."

"Wow," my daughter said. "How dramatic. Why do you have to always be so dramatic?"

"I don't think not wanting to feel like a possession is dramatic," I said in a manner that seems, now, in hindsight, admittedly, a little dramatic.

"I'm going upstairs," my daughter said.

I walked around a series of empty rooms not feeling like anyone's possession. It didn't feel as good as I thought.

Miley Cyrus

I was heart broken and I couldn't shit.
It was one, two o'clock in the morning.
I could feel the shit, hard and pellet-like, up in there, up inside of my rectum,
But it wouldn't come out.
(I had been sitting there a long time.)
I was staring at a picture of Miley Cyrus's tits in *Paper* magazine.
I wrapped my middle finger in a wipe and shoved it up my ass,
Felt around, located the hard balls of shit and pulled some out.
I wrapped my finger in a fresh wipe and pulled again.
I could feel my butthole ease up,
And more shit ready to come out, on its own, without me pulling.
I was still heart broken but at least now I could shit.
Miley Cyrus had someone's name tattooed under her left tit.
I couldn't make it out.
It looked like it started with a 'J.'
Jesse or Justin or Jamey.
I had a tattoo of a buffalo on my right rib.
The buffalo may as well be my husband's name.
I didn't know if Miley Cyrus had ever been constipated.
I pictured her having a bleached asshole.
I pictured her asshole being nice and tight and pink.

Party (2013)

It was a hot Saturday in July.

I was inside a motel room in Findlay (Ohio).

My daughter was gone for the day, scuba-diving for certification in a quarry somewhere
near by.

I'd brought my swimsuit too.

There was a photograph of an outdoor pool on the motel website.

But when I walked outside to look at it, it was small and in the middle of the parking lot.

The water was a color I'd never seen before.

There was a slick baby oil sheen floating on top

And a man standing next to his truck nearby, spitting.

I sat on the bed in our room instead.

I could see Walmart and Cracker Barrel from the window.

I read half of *Wallcreeper* and both introductions to *Tropic of Cancer*.

I wrote notes to myself (or to someone else) in my notebook.

(Nothing publishable either way.)

By noon I was feeling stir crazy.

I ate a protein bar and looked out the window at the Waffle House across the street.

I counted the hours 'til my daughter would be back: six.

I thought about walking to the Walmart but the Walmart was on the other side of the
freeway overpass.

I couldn't make out a sidewalk on the overpass.

I imagined myself walking on the shoulder of the road while men in trucks shouted
things at me and spat.

I decided not to go to Walmart.

I looked around some more.

On the same side of the overpass I was on was a high school and running in front of the
high school was a sidewalk.

I figured I would walk half an hour up the sidewalk and then turn around and walk half
an hour back.

A walk of the privileged class!

It was cold in the motel room from the air conditioning.

Outside on the asphalt it was ninety degrees.

I started to sweat almost immediately.

It felt like waking up.

I bought a water bottle at the gas station before crossing the street.

A guy sitting on the curb with a toddler seemed to say something to me and spit.

I walked fast like I was in a hurry to get somewhere even though we both could tell I had
nowhere I needed to get.

On the corner while waiting for the light to change I spat.

I walked past the high school and I walked past houses.
There was a house that said it was an antique store and a house that said it was a hair salon and a building that had once sold car parts but was now for sale.
Then there were no more houses and I was walking along a two lane highway up a hill and at the top of the hill was a park and a cemetery.
The cemetery had big shade trees and I figured I'd cool off a minute before heading back.

I was listening to a playlist on my iPod I'd named 'party 2013.'
'party 2013' contained 82 songs by Mariah Carey and Cobra Starship and Missy Elliott and Bobby Brown and I listened to it on airplanes and when I took walks around my neighborhood at night.

I couldn't remember having a party in 2013.

I was in the oldest section of the cemetery, which contained most of the shade trees.

The gravestones in the oldest section had quotes like "grow old with me! The best is yet to be, the last of life, for which the first was made" and inscriptions that said nice things like "a gracious lady" and "a just man of keen intellect."

"Party in the U.S.A." was playing on my iPod.

I couldn't imagine anyone using the word 'gracious' or 'lady' to describe me.

I didn't know anyone who would quote Robert Browning to me either (in life or death).

Side by side were a pair of headstones that read "a kind and thoughtful lady, librarian and teacher" and "and above all, a gentleman."

There were several small headstones on which the years of birth and death were four or less years apart.

On one of those headstones was a carving of a lamb and under it the name Eleanor.

I remembered six years earlier walking through a graveyard at night with my daughter and her friends.

I had parked a few blocks away in case we were caught trespassing at night and on the walk back to the car a woman in a minivan had rolled down her window to ask if we needed a ride.

"I'm a mom," she had said. "It's safe."

I was a mom too but I was dressed like a teenager, the same way I was dressed in the
Findlay cemetery.

I had been in love with a man fourteen years younger than me in 2009.

'Now That We Found Love' was playing on my iPod.

I was walking back toward the freeway.

There was a long rectangular plot of land with a modern-looking headstone in the middle
of it and a park bench across from the headstone.

I stopped to read the headstone.

It said 'Andrew Guglielmi: 1980-2000', and I stood there wondering how a twenty year
old might die: drug overdose, car crash, suicide . . .

I walked on, out of the cemetery, along the freeway.
The sun was behind me now and soon I could feel a puddle of sweat forming on my back.
I used my t-shirt to soak it up.
There were three songs by Katy Perry in a row and I was grateful for them.
By the time I reached the corner on which my motel sat I was starving.
I went into the McDonald's and bought a hamburger and an iced coffee and sat in a booth
alone with my earbuds still in ("Irreplaceable" was playing on my iPod).
Imagining what it would be like to live in Findlay, Ohio . . .

(I was romanticizing small town living again now that I no longer lived in one.)

Later I looked up the name of the boy whose gravestone I had seen.
There was a magazine article about spring break accidents in which he was included: a
drunken fall from a third floor balcony in Panama City, Florida.

Somehow the reality of his death was less romantic than I'd made it in my head and I
apologized to him, silently, for trying to make it romantic.

Yesterday

I was sitting in a hair salon waiting for my daughter to get her hair cut. There were magazines stacked on a table in front of me and on the cover of the top magazine was a photograph of Kloe Kardashian and I didn't have any interest in reading about or looking at photographs of Kloe Kardashian even if she had lost weight so I took out my phone to text Tanja instead.

Do you ever feel like your life is like *Groundhog Day*? I said.

You mean like déjà vu, Tanja said.

No, like every year it's the same pattern and meaningless, I said.

Sounds dreary, Tanja said.

Yeah, I said. It didn't seem like Tanja ever felt that way.

Later my daughter asked if she could play me EDM music in the car. She had just bought tickets for an EDM concert. I said, "Are you going to take molly?" And she said, "Probably not." And I said, "Why not? I think you should." And she said, "I feel like if I took it now I would just feel guilty and I want to wait until a time when I won't feel guilty." I wanted to tell her there would never be a time in which she didn't feel guilty if she felt guilty now but the music was about ready to drop and I wanted to concentrate on that so I stopped talking. Part of me regretted not taking more drugs. "Besides," my daughter said (she wasn't waiting for the drop). "You never know what you're getting. Look at Luna, she thought she was taking molly and later she found out she'd taken crystal meth." "Yeah," I said. I'd missed the drop but somehow I still felt better. "I think the EDM music is making me feel better," I said. My daughter laughed. "That's good," she said. "It's really uplifting," I said. "Yeah," she said. It didn't seem like she ever felt that way either.

I always feel like I am waiting now for what I've heard referred to as an 'aha!' moment so I will know what to do but the 'aha!' moment never arrives and instead I am inundated with a lot of smaller 'hmmm' moments that don't add up to much and so I don't do anything or make any decisions.

Maybe, though, I have had an 'aha!' moment or a series of 'aha!' moments, even, and have not recognized them as such because I do not actually want to make decisions or to leave my room or to leave my bed or something.

Or maybe I am just waiting for someone to text me and everything I wrote above this is asking you to do that for me now please.

BBW

I think the way people define 'love' and define 'obsession' (or distinguish between the two) has more to do with how things turn out for them, like, if they turn out 'good' or 'bad,' I.e. if they end up 'together' or married vs. if they end up writing a book about someone with whom they are no longer in contact, than with anything else—like actual feelings or emotions or whatever—which seems unfair or inaccurate or something.

Like, they will put you in a mental hospital for one thing but not the other, I mean.

Chris Brown

I was having another gathering at my house.

Seven of us were seated around a round table in the center of my living room.

I knew five of the six other people fairly well.

The sixth person I had met once before, in passing, and now he was sleeping

On an air mattress in my basement.

(Earlier in the day he had clogged a toilet.)

(Currently he was drinking something called a Rye-and-Gosling.)

We were playing some sort of card game.

The sixth person was playing music through his iPhone on my speakers.

A song I didn't have time to recognize came on and the sixth person said, "We don't listen
    to Chris Brown in this house" and the song changed.

Oh, now I remember: we were eating carry out pizza.

Suddenly I felt sick. I didn't feel like eating anymore.

I said, "So we're part of the 'do something once and get labeled for life' vibe?"

The sixth man said, "He beat the shit out of Rihanna."

"And then she got back with him," I said.

"And then he destroyed the Today show dressing room," the sixth man said.

"Those incidents were both five or six years ago," I said.

"I can't support a man who beats women," the sixth man said.

"Sounds like Twitter," I said.

(I should have said, "Then don't listen to The Beatles. Don't listen to John Lennon.")

I was standing and I carried my paper plate to the garbage can and dropped it in.

I didn't know where to go after that or what to do so I kept walking.

I walked down the hall to my bedroom.

I walked through my bedroom to my bathroom.

I sat on the edge of my tub with my head in my hands.

I thought I might still throw up.

I sat there a while and when I didn't throw up, I sat in my closet and cried.

I wasn't sure why I was crying.

I felt like an asshole crying for Chris Brown.

Maybe I was crying for myself and that made me more of an asshole, but I couldn't stop.

I thought of *The Scarlet Letter* and I thought of the witch trials and I thought of
    homosexuals being fired from their jobs for sodomy and I thought of being raised to
    believe in redemption and second chances and (the teachings of) Buddha or Jesus or
    Dr. King.

I thought about how every week a different person was vilified on social media, how my
    father had beat my mother and she had left him and then how she'd gone on to
    date another man who had beat her off and on for years. I thought about how the
    two of them had been arrested for beating each other outside the bar where they
    worked. I thought about my mother physically assaulting me and me physically

assaulting my first real boyfriend when I was nineteen. I thought about how if we give women the benefit of the doubt (or make excuses for them) for staying in an abusive relationship, we have to give men the benefit of the doubt also. I thought about Rihanna saying, "Damn, you'd think you were the one who got your ass beat," on Twitter when someone scolded her for getting back with Chris.

I thought about the video I'd watched recently of Chris Brown dancing with his daughter and how it seemed not unreasonable to believe that he was trying to turn his life around/trying to be a good father/trying not to be an asshole.

I thought about how some people didn't want that to ever happen; how some people were invested in Chris Brown being vilified, in how that made them feel about themselves, comparatively.

A part of me didn't ever want to leave my closet.

But then the sixth man came into my bedroom to find me.
The sixth man found me in my closet, crying.

I stood up. I knew what he was going to say; I was preparing myself to hear it.

I heard the sixth man saying things and then I heard myself saying, "I just don't think you can have empathy for anyone if you don't attempt to have empathy for everyone."

I heard myself say, "Chris Brown is trying to be a good dad."
I heard myself say, "Chris Brown is a human being."

I knew even as I said these things, what a good story this would make for the sixth man (to tell about me) later.

I knew how I would tell it.

"And then she started crying over Chris Brown," I would say.
"Who the fuck cries about Chris Brown?" I would say. Big laugh.

It would be a great story to tell.
I thought the sixth man should thank me for giving him such a great story.

Instead he sat back down around the round table and I sat, reclined, in a nearby chair with an ashtray on my stomach, smoking.

The sliding glass door was ajar.

It was my house and I was smoking with the door ajar.

And it was September, 2015.

Everyone keeps telling me I am a 'strong vibrant woman'/ please stop telling me I'm a strong woman please

Tanja texted me that today:
"You're a strong vibrant woman," she said.
I didn't reply.
I was on my bathroom floor sobbing into a hand towel as usual.

Ultimatum

Whenever someone attempts to give me an ultimatum, I realize very quickly that the person has given him/herself an ultimatum, and I wait, with 'vested interest,' to see what option he/she will choose regarding it.

Miley Cyrus II

Maybe I loved him too much and that's why I couldn't stop hurting him.
(I told myself there had to be a reasonable explanation for why I kept hurting him.)
I just kept hurting him
& hurting him & I hurt too because of hurting him.

I stared at Miley Cyrus.
The pull quote beneath her bared breasts said she didn't judge anyone.

It felt good knowing Miley didn't judge me for hurting him.

Tanja

Tanja says, "You have a lot of pop culture references in these poems."

Tanja says, "I started to get annoyed with all the pop culture references while I was
    reading your poems."

"But I guess that's the point," Tanja says.

"Mmmhmm," I say, even though I don't ever know what the point is.

Tanja likes Hanson and Matchbox Twenty.

Tanja has a Nicki Minaj brand shirt she got at Kmart before our last tour.

I can't remember the last time I felt drunk.
Last night I didn't smoke a cigarette even though I was alone.

BOB DYLAN SONGS

(June, 2016–November, 2016)

Therapeutic Riding Center

In January we began receiving emails—
a new practice they decided to implement

Background checks for all volunteers

To make sure we weren't on the terrorist watch list or list of sex offenders

"It's a decision the board made," the email said. "For everyone's safety"

We had been walking beside horses, holding onto the legs of children and young adults
and senior citizens, three hours a night, two nights a week, for two years

My daughter had been a volunteer for three years before that

We weren't on the terrorist watch list or list of sex offenders but someone close to us was

We said we weren't going to consent to a background check because we objected to
background checks and to the sex offenders' list for moral reasons

The board said we had to, that it was just the ways things were now

We were at a standoff

(unfinished)

Animal Sanctuary

I.

I started volunteering at an animal sanctuary after the therapeutic riding place didn't work out

My daughter's friend told me about it
My daughter's friend mowed lawns and did carpentry at the animal sanctuary
He wrote an email recommending me

The animal sanctuary was split into two divisions as far as caretaking: mammal and herps. The herps were reptiles and amphibians. Herpetology.
But I called them reptiles because I always forgot the word herpetology.

When I came home from a day spent volunteering I would tell my husband stories.

"Wait," he would say. "Is [so-and-so] a 'mammal person' or a 'reptile person'?"

Even though I had told him several times almost everyone there was a mammal person.

Only Simon and James and I were reptile people.

There were fifteen to twenty thin young women who didn't wear make up and had long, straight brown hair who volunteered with the mammals. Once, I walked into a room in which they were all sitting, waiting for a meeting, and I thought they could easily have been mistaken for Manson family members.

I got out of that room soon as I could.

I didn't interact much with the mammal people.

II.

James taught me how to do everything at the sanctuary: soak the Russian tortoises, mist the iguanas, pick up the Solomon Island and blue-tongued skinks, hand-feed crickets to the axolotls and fire salamanders, moisten the giant toads.

I worked two days a week and each day I worked I made a giant salad for all the plant eaters.

I started by picking wild dandelions from the field behind the barn in appropriate weather.

After that I went around the giant tortoises yard and picked up their shit. It was large—about the length of a tallboy—and smelled barnyard'y, which in my mind meant it smelled good. I wore a plastic bag over my hand to pick up each giant turd, dropped them one by one into a larger plastic bag.

Sometimes the smaller tortoise followed me around the yard, ran after me, charged me when I filled the water dish, tried to climb into it. The smaller tortoise's name was Hank. When James was with me he would say, "Hank, stop being an asshole. Hank, why are you such a douche?"

James was my age, extremely knowledgeable, extremely chatty. But James didn't get along with the man who ran the sanctuary, so James wasn't there a lot. James trained me and then James sort of took a step back.

Which meant I had to interact with Simon. Simon was twenty-four, twenty-five, quiet, passive aggressive, and uninterested in me. He was medium height, extremely thin, with glasses. He looked like Bill Haverchuck on *Freaks and Geeks*. Which was a shame because I'd always loved Bill Haverchuck and now it seemed like Bill Haverchuck hated me.

I would pass Simon on the path between buildings and say hi and Simon would keep walking as though he hadn't heard me.

The problem was Simon was sort of in charge of me. There were only three paid employees at the sanctuary and James and Simon were two of them. The third was a friendly, good-natured young man from Australia, Zed. Unfortunately, Zed worked mostly with the mammals. I would overhear Zed speaking with one of the Manson mammal girls in his friendly Australian accent, joking around with her, smiling a lot, as they made food for the kangaroos or sloth, and look over at Simon, staring silently at his phone as he ate an entire pizza, never once looking up at me, and wonder what it was about me Simon hated.

III.

The iguanas, like most of the animals at the sanctuary, were rescues.

The male was donated when his owner couldn't afford the operation he needed to remove a large growth on his face.

Later I learned the owner had asked for him back, after the operation was successful, and it kind of broke my heart that they wouldn't give the iguana back to him since 23 ½ hours a day the iguana was alone in a closet they'd converted to an enclosure, which meant it had one tiny window at the top of the door. As soon as I unlocked it I would hear him get down from his log perch and run over to the door and scratch for me to open it. Eventually James showed me it was okay to leave the door open, let him wander around the hall as I cleaned his enclosure and brought him his salad and water.

All he ever seemed to want was to see what I was doing and to have me bend down and pet him.

I knew he was so tame on account of the man who had raised him. I regretted being told about the man asking for him back. I wondered if I could offer to pay whatever the surgery had cost so the man could have him again but I didn't know how long it'd been, if the man was still alive, still able to care for him.

More honestly, I was a coward, afraid to make waves at the sanctuary, afraid people would hate me if I brought it up. So instead I tried to spend a little extra time petting the male iguana and letting him walk around the hallway outside his enclosure before locking the door again for the day.

I think this added to Simon's dislike of me. I think he saw it as a waste of time, when there were so many other jobs to do, so many more enclosures to clean, reptiles and amphibians to feed.

The female had been found wandering the diag at the university, most likely a discarded pet of a college student. She was my favorite because no one else at the sanctuary liked her. Even Zed rolled his eyes when I told him she was my favorite.

"She has soulful eyes," I would say and he would laugh and repeat, "'Soulful eyes.' No, no, she's evil. Pure evil," in his adorable Australian accent.

She was as timid and reserved as the male iguana was outgoing and friendly and I saw her as a challenge. I designated myself "the iguana whisperer," and worked patiently at winning her over, at getting her to remember and trust me. I spent extra time misting her, which she seemed to enjoy, closing her eyes as the fine particles of water fell by the hundreds onto her face and head, and brought her stalks of mustard and collard greens which I picked up from Whole Foods as a special treat on my way to the sanctuary.

I tried to do all this "iguana whispering" when Simon was busy in another part of the sanctuary or on his day off, which coincided with one of the days I volunteered.

I had seen the bites and scratches she'd given James when he'd had to gather her for a vet visit. I'd stood outside her enclosure, a closet next to the male's, out of sight but within hearing distance, listening to the thrashings

IV.

I'd been working at the animal sanctuary twice a week for six months when they held their annual fundraiser. The year before my husband and I had attended as paying guests. I remembered Simon walking around with one of the Solomon Island skinks on his arm. I remember asking him questions about it, him answering me like a normal person.

"They are unique in the reptile world in that they give birth to live babies rather than laying eggs."

The annual fundraiser was a dinner followed by a presentation of animals. The fundraiser was held in conjunction with a large zoo from a neighboring state. Every year the zoo sent two human representatives with four or five animals. The presentation at the fundraiser would be a mix of animals from the sanctuary and animals from the zoo.

For weeks before the fundraiser everyone at the sanctuary was rushing about, cleaning every inch of the sanctuary that would be visible to the guests, hanging multiple reams of fly paper, setting a large number of roach traps, finally throwing out all the spoiled vegetables and fruit that had been rotting in bins for weeks.

As shitty as Simon was at interpersonal relationships, he was that much a hard worker. In the weeks leading up to the fundraiser he worked seven days a week, I don't know how many hours a day. Ten? Twelve?

It was admirable, how dedicated he was to his job. But it sucked how he seemed to take out his frustrations with how much he was working on me.

He seemed to forget or not care that I was an unpaid employee.

He seemed to think I should be staying more hours in the weeks leading up to the fundraiser because he was.

At the same time, volunteers were quitting.

I was the only consistent reptile volunteer at this point.

Every day I tended to the same chores and almost every day Simon would text me to ask if I'd had time to take on new ones and seem disappointed when I hadn't.

It was starting to wear me down.

One day I walked down the stairs into the basement and heard Simon talking about me to James.

"She's always marking that she cleaned the salamanders. What does that *mean*? I don't get why she keeps checking that she's cleaning the salamanders?"

I thought Simon was mistaken or that I'd mistakenly checked the box for cleaning the salamanders instead of the box for cleaning the axolotls.

I didn't understand why Simon wouldn't speak to me directly.

I walked back up the stairs, fed crickets to the clawed frogs in the sink until Simon and James exited the basement, rather than confronting them.

The night of the fundraiser I was stationed outside with the giant tortoises. I'd been given a fact sheet about them and was to talk to guests as they made their way from the parking lot to the main building. It was September and getting darker earlier. It was 6:45, past the time the tortoises normally went into their shed-sized building for the night.

I'd gotten the smallest of the three tortoises outside but the other two weren't budging.

Simon and Zed walked by and I waved them over, explained the situation. Zed smiled at me as usual, offered to carry them out. Simon didn't say anything to me directly but helped Zed lift the tortoises, joking around and calling them "assholes" as they stumbled carrying them outside to the grass.

For thirty minutes I stood in the tortoise yard answering questions about their eating habits and place of origin and lifespan. By then everyone had arrived and I went inside the main building to help Darcy with the Gila monster and the ball python and the pancake tortoises. I'd been given fact sheets on them, too.

I'd met Darcy my first week working at the sanctuary, though I hadn't seen her much that summer. Unlike the young Manson mammal women she was short and chubby and wore glasses and spoke to me.

The first day I met her she complimented me on my Nirvana T-shirt.

"Did I ever tell you the names I gave the fire salamanders?" she asked me when there was a lull in the fundraising crowd.

"No," I said. "You didn't."

"I named each of them after a different character on *Always Sunny*," she said. And then she began to list each salamander's name and what characteristic about it had caused her to name it that.

I liked her because unlike most everyone else at the sanctuary, she was easy to talk to and because she seemed to be able to talk to Simon, too. She didn't seem to notice how odd he was and it seemed like he liked her or didn't hate her or something.

After the guests went into the arena to eat their dinner, I stood with Darcy in the area "backstage" as she talked with Simon and James and Zed. I thought maybe her acceptance of me, as well as Zed's and James's, would rub off on Simon. Simon was holding a can of beer, which seemed like a promising sign.

I'd heard rumors of Simon drunk at the Christmas party the year before.

We stood—the five of us—in a circle, joking about Simon's drinking and figuring out a way he could continue drinking without the higher ups knowing. It felt conspiratorial, in a good way, because for once it felt like I was on the inside of the conspiracy.

"I got it," Zed said in his cheery Australian accent. "Give me that beer, I'll be right back."

He ran off to the kitchen, returning two minutes later with a Coke can in which he had poured Simon's beer.

"Brilliant," Simon said.

I stood opposite Simon, smiling. Encouraging.

As the presentation began Darcy and I made our way into the area reserved for volunteers and sat on the end of the bleachers, near the Manson mammal women. James and Zed stood beside us. Simon was onstage holding a large stick from which a sloth was hanging as his boss, Roger, talked with the audience about sloth behavior.

When it was the zoo's turn to present, Simon came and stood with James and Zed beside us and made jokes about Roger, who was still onstage, now wearing a cowboy hat sideways for a presentation with a sugar glider who would jump from the zoo employee's shoulder onto Roger's head.

"Why is Roger wearing the hat sideways? Does he think he's a pirate?" Simon said, sipping his Coke can, and the four of us laughed.

The rest of the night was an alternation of watching Simon handling animals with Roger on stage and listening to Simon and James trade jokes about Roger and the animals.

By the time I left that night I felt a lot better about everything, and about my role at the sanctuary.

I felt like there had been some sort of breakthrough in my relationship with Simon, like I was part of the 'in crowd' now. Like maybe he would stop being an asshole to me.

I was glad I'd decided to buy the conservancy shirt I was wearing for five dollars rather than just borrow it for the night.

v.

The Monday following the fundraiser I received a text from Simon on my way in to work.

"I'm not coming in today," it said. "Do your usual tasks and also feed the box turtles if you can. James should be there if you need help."

I'd never fed the box turtles before. I wasn't even sure where they were located.

I sent Simon a text in reply, "Ok, sounds good."

Then, because of how well I thought things had gone Friday night at the fundraiser, I decided I'd try a small joke.

"Are you still hungover from Friday night?"

I included a smiley face so he would know I was kidding.

I left my phone in the car and walked to the giant tortoise yard to start picking up their shit.

Halfway through my shift I needed something from my car. I'd forgotten the kale and mustard greens I'd brought for the iguanas. While I was at the car I decided to check my phone to see if Simon had replied.

There was a text from him but all it said was, "I was never drunk on Friday."

No smiley face.

I immediately felt dejected. Nothing seemed to have changed at all. I had been a fool to believe it had.

Even though nothing had changed, I felt worse than I had before because now I had had the three days to think things were going to be better.

I closed my car door and walked inside to feed the iguanas.

I stood at the kitchen counter chopping an apple.

It was unusually quiet because most people had taken the day off after weeks of working long hours in preparation for the fundraiser.

Roger was in his office with the older woman who fed the parrots. The older woman was named Dorothy and Dorothy always called me "honey" and was kind in the way a woman in her sixties with no children and a houseful of parrots and a husband who sleeps upright in a chair in the living room because he has a feeding tube and can't lie flat on his back anymore is kind. Dorothy was helping Roger clean his office, which was covered in owl shit from the owl he'd adopted at the beginning of summer and allowed free range of his office and kitchen.

Once the owl had landed on my back when I was alone washing dishes. I'd been watching it nervously over my shoulder for half an hour. I didn't like the feeling of it being behind me. I'd turned to see it running across the floor toward me. I remember worrying it would attack my ankles. I didn't think it would jump on my back.

I was wearing a tank top and its talons were digging into my shoulders.

I tried saying "step off" and sidling up to the counter and to his perch as I'd seen Simon do but he wouldn't budge.

I'd radioed for Simon for help and Simon had replied from some other building, "Stand up."

Eventually I got the owl to "step off" onto Roger's desk. I closed the door to Roger's office and rubbed my shoulders.

Now Roger had moved the owl to a permanent enclosure near the arena. Someone said he had landed on another volunteer's head.

Dorothy came out to dump a bucket.

"Who you makin' salad for today, honey?" she said.

I told her I was making salad for the iguanas and she said, "Are they your favorite animals here?" and I said yes. We talked for a few minutes about the iguanas and the parrots and her dead horses buried in the field behind her house and about her husband's stomach and feeding tube and I didn't understand why Simon and I couldn't talk like that, what it was about me Simon found so annoying or off-putting.

Later I was washing dishes when Roger asked Dorothy to open the doors so he could walk the horse through the kitchen.

I should have realized the prophetic nature of the moment.

The last time Roger had walked the horse through the kitchen when I was working was during my first week at the sanctuary. I remembered thinking how exciting it was to work in a building where horses and emus and mountain lions passed through the kitchen.

I remembered thinking how lucky I was to get to work there.

Dorothy handed the horse a cucumber.

"Cucumber? For a horse? That's a first," Roger said.

"If you ever have an inkling to let an owl have free range of your office, Elizabeth, don't," Roger said.

I smiled. There were bits of horse slobber and cucumber on the floor and Dorothy and I stooped to wipe them up.

VI.

My final minutes at the sanctuary were spent feeding the box turtles in Roger's yard with James.

I'd never been to Roger's yard before. I didn't even know his house was right next door.

James had carried over two blue plastic containers of earthworms and we stood around two large child's swimming pools filled with dirt and turtles, feeding them. We carried the water containers to the side of Roger's house, dumped them and refilled them from the faucet.

I was learning a new task on what I didn't realize was my last day.

"I know Simon hates me," I said and I told James about our text exchange.

I was hoping James would say, "No, he doesn't" or "Oh, that's just Simon being sarcastic."

Instead he said something like, "Simon has a hard time relating to older people. He doesn't like this one other older woman either. It's easier for Simon to talk to people his age."

I knew James was trying to make me feel better but he was only making me feel worse.

I didn't normally think much about my age. I had friends of all ages. It had never been an issue. Suddenly I felt ashamed of being older. I loathed myself for not being in my twenties so Simon could more easily relate to me.

I hadn't sat and thought about how I was the only regular unpaid employee not in my twenties.

I suddenly felt like Simon was right to be off put by me. I thought maybe all along I had been a source of conversation and speculation. *What is she even doing here at her age?*

I stopped on my drive home for a coffee. As I got back in my car I suddenly burst into tears. I think I knew then I would never go back.

VII.

I kept seeing the faces of the animals I'd worked with everywhere I went.

I have a hard time letting go of people.

There were twenty-one smaller tortoises—The Russians and pancakes—in the basement in five different bins.

Every day I had begun my shift at the sanctuary by soaking twenty-one tortoises and cleaning their bins.

It took an hour and a half.

Toward the end of the summer I had started bringing heads of romaine lettuce with me to feed the tortoises once they were done soaking and their bins were cleaned.

So they didn't have to wait for me to make the salad and bring some back for them at the end of my shift.

They always acted as though they were famished. As soon as I entered the large closet in which their bins were housed they ran down to the end of their bin in which they were fed.

They peered up at me. Six or seven heads to a bin. Twelve or fourteen eyes all watching me.

The last time I'd soaked them I'd noticed how dirty their undersides were, caked with feces.

I'd gotten paper towels and wiped the shit from their bottom shells before returning them each to their bin. On average I used three squares of paper towel on each tortoise's underside.

I would not have predicted the tortoises would be the animals I most missed when I no longer worked there.

They were the most commonplace, the least exotic.
You could buy them at any pet store for twenty bucks.

But there was something so satisfying watching them eat the food I brought them. There was a vulnerability to lifting them one at a time out of the water, turds floating around them. Peering into their little faces. Returning them to a clean home.

I had brought my daughter with me one day over the summer to help me and to see the animals. She had been surprised I was so willing to put my hands in water filled with shit. She was a marine biology major and she wouldn't put her hands in the water. "I will someday when that's my paid job but I'm not doing it for free."

I smiled up at her, lifting another tortoise out of the water. It didn't bother me at all.

I knew it was the coolest opportunity I, a woman without a college degree in my forties, would ever have.

I felt so proud to take my daughter with me through my routine that day, to show her all my chores.

I didn't think it'd be the last time.

I waited until two in the morning the night before my next shift to send an email to the person in charge of volunteers to tell her I wasn't going to be coming in any more.

I had been unable all weekend to make a decision.

I don't think I realized how heartbroken I would be until I hit "send."

Couples Therapy — Nathan for You

Our first couples' therapist had a cheesy website or a cheesy internet presence

It said he specialized in *men's issues*
It didn't say much about his education

But we had to start somewhere

My husband and I had been living apart for eight months
I was about to go on tour, about to see a man I'd been unable to let go of, *emotionally*, even though I hadn't seen the man in six years

(or, at least, this is how we're taught to label such relationships in places like couples therapy, inside of marriages, I mean)

My husband kept saying he thought we were going to get a divorce
I didn't know what I thought

The man had asked me to publish his book
The man had asked to read with my tour mates and me when we came to his city on tour
The man had said it was important to him that we remain friends

I had told my husband all this
Or most of it

I asked my tour mates about the ethics of publishing this man's book and about the ethics of allowing this man to read with us

My tour mates, being *artists*, told me I should do whatever felt right, not to repress myself

I had been referring to marriage as an act of codependency for months

My husband hated when I used that term to describe our relationship

"But I don't think we are special in that regard," I said. "I think marriage in general is inherently codependent. All long term relationships are, by nature."

Our first couples' therapist didn't see it that way

He said, "You can not be friends with this man. You have to give him up at once"

This was ten minutes into our first and final session with this therapist
It was the first time in ten minutes the therapist had looked at our acknowledged me
Or spoken to me

Prior to this he had only spoken to and acknowledged my husband

Men's issues

"Well," I said to my husband. "There you go. Isn't this the point of our being here?"

After that the therapist had my husband and me turn toward one another on the couch and hold hands so my husband could look me in the eye and tell me how sad I made him.

It all felt so horribly manipulative and I was sure my husband felt validated.

Earlier in the session, the therapist had asked my husband what emotion he felt when he thought of me and when my husband didn't answer the therapist had said, "Well, there are really only three emotions: happy, sad and angry."

So my husband had said, "I don't know, then, angry?"

And the therapist had said, "Anger is always a mask for a deeper emotion. So pick another one."

"Sad?" my husband had said.

I was rolling my eyes in my head. I felt like I was on a bad TV show. *Candid Camera*, maybe.

Which was when I finally realized who the therapist reminded me of

I'd been trying to place him the entire session

In between hearing about how shitty I was

But now I had to sit and stare at my husband while he nonverbally communicated his sadness to me in a drafty basement office

So I waited until we were outside on the sidewalk to tell him

"Oh yeah," my husband said. "I can totally see that."

"Maybe his whole psych 101 chatter was a gag," I said.

"Maybe," my husband said.

"I don't think I can take him seriously," I said.

"Yeah," my husband said.

"We'll keep looking," I said. "When I get back from tour."

"Okay," my husband said.

My husband had already told me he wasn't going to talk to me while I was away on tour.

I was to be gone ten days.

We had an appointment with another therapist three days after my return.

I don't remember ever believing we were going to get a divorce

But "divorce" was also just another man-made concept, another word, like "marriage" and "fidelity" and "sad"—it didn't matter ultimately to my inner self whether we were married or divorced because either way I was still me

This was how cynically I was thinking then

There's only so much blame you can take before you start turning it back around
—Eugene O'Neill

I was feeling "manipulated" but then I was aware that itself was just another made up concept, another word to get what you wanted or to turn the tables or to exonerate yourself or to vilify another person

It was starting to feel impossible to believe anything mattered

It was becoming increasingly easy to believe nothing did

My husband and I went to dinner

I don't remember where

I don't remember what we said

And then I went on tour

Couples Therapy II

Our second couples' therapist was my grandfather's age and had a Ph.D.

His office was on the sixth floor of the tallest building in the city

You had to be buzzed into the building, take an elevator up

It felt like a building in which a scene with a psychiatrist would be filmed in a Woody Allen movie

Which validated it in my mind

The waiting room was tiny, more like a Wes Anderson set, with tiny chairs and a tiny end table on which *The New Yorker* and *The Sun* magazines were stacked, red carpet and wood paneling, a box of Kleenex

It was hard for my husband and me to maneuver within the tiny waiting room

You could not, for instance, remove your coat without major shuffling, so we sat with our coasts on waiting for the psychiatrist to come retrieve us

The main office was, at least comparatively, large and sprawling

The state of Texas as compared to Rhode Island

Persian rugs laid strategically over carpet, an assortment of tables and table lamps, waste baskets and boxes of Kleenex, a white couch that did not get used aside from holding my draped coat, and a large window with a view to our backs or to my periphery from where I sat in a chair across from the psychiatrist and an end table from my husband

It was quite a comfortable room, in keeping with the Woody Allen film vibe

It felt very New York "intellectual" for a small Midwestern university city

Prior to the first couples' therapist, I had seen independently a therapist, once, six years earlier, for approximately eight sessions but she, like the first couples' therapist, had not inspired me, had seemed dull and dimwitted and focused on what I considered "the wrong things (my mother, my mother, my mother!)"

Dr. X, as I'll call him, seemed smarter and exemplified this right away by not focusing on the man I should or shouldn't talk to, but on less titillating issues, such as my daughter having left home for college the autumn prior and the literary scandal in which I'd found myself a key player during that same time period and my husband's reaction or non-reaction to both, his support or non-support of me during that time

I found myself, that initial session, in reluctant tears, as I had been in the hours leading up to the session, a result of coming off tour and of the continuing effects of the scandal and of missing my daughter, and of digesting the fresh awareness that I probably wasn't ever going to talk to the man in question again

At one point during this visit I remember Dr. X referring to Lee (my husband) as "cerebral and cool," saying, "even if you were busy, sadness has a way of permeating at the cracks" which was in response to Lee saying he had been too busy with academic work to feel sad about Eli (my daughter) leaving the house for college the previous fall

It was an interesting observation for me, my husband's emotional numbness, whether it was a mask or not, it had surely played as much a part of our separation as the question of whether or not I talked to the other man and I was certain both were intertwined and encouraging of the other

I felt equally unsupported by Lee's inability to stand up for me in the initial days and weeks of the scandal

"We had agreed," I told the psychiatrist. "That his saying anything wouldn't do any good, but then at some point I didn't care the effect and only wanted my husband to be so overcome by emotion on my behalf that he said something anyway, even if it didn't make intellectual sense to do so"

"Yes," Dr. X said. "We cannot address all dumb things said, that would be our entire life, but in this case, you wife was directly attacked"

It was a similar reaction my husband's best friend had when we explained the scandal and its aftermath to him

My husband's best friend who is a pastor had said, "And what did you do?"

"Nothing," my husband had said. "I didn't do anything"

I could see the look of surprise on the face of my Lee's best friend

I had told him anonymous people had sent me messages telling me they felt sorry for my daughter, that I was her mother

If I was the scapegoat of the first couples therapy session, my husband must have felt himself more examined in this one

Afterward we took the elevator to the basement where there were public bathrooms

We stood in the hall, leaning on large bins for garbage and recycling

"I liked him," I said. "I feel like I could talk to him on a whole assortment of philosophical issues."

"I was glad you initiated the conversation this time," my husband said. "This was definitely harder," he said

We stood there a while, facing one another

I thought my husband might have tears in his eyes or maybe he was yawning

"I just feel so drained," he said

"Let's get something to eat," I said

We weren't supposed to try to continue therapy outside of the office

We were supposed to save any anger that arose throughout the week, also

It was starting to snow as we walked along the sidewalk toward the restaurant we had decided on

It was only 4:30; Happy Hour

Almost Thanksgiving

Couples Therapy III

We saw the second couples' therapist every Tuesday at 3:30 for the next four months

I dressed for therapy as though I was Mia Farrow in *Alice*, even though I would only wear the clothes for an hour, perhaps two if we went to dinner after, and then would change back into pajamas or sweatpants

I wore my gold necklace and my gold ring and my wool sweaters and my gabardine pants

For the most part, being a narcissist, I enjoyed the whole production, the introspection and examination, until eventually the questions took on a repetitive nature, and it began to feel as though we were treading water rather than uncovering any new truths

Lee seemed to sweat every session

We spent the majority of the first four sessions waiting for Lee to answer questions

"I'm unused to talking about these things," he would tell me after.
"You have all your friends you talk to all the time. I have no one," he said.

"You have me," I said

"*I have you*," Lee repeated. "But that doesn't help me much when you're what I need to talk about"

"Oh," I said

It was the middle of February when therapy started to feel like picking a scab

I had told Lee the week before that I felt we had gotten what we needed out of going; we seemed to have run out of real issues to talk about

But Lee had said the last two sessions had felt most beneficial to him, so I let it go

But I became resentful; I refused to be the one to start the conversation

Previously we had taken turns

We would stand in the tiny Wes Anderson waiting room discussing who would start and with what

In hindsight, this may have been one of the cons of our therapy; Dr. X seemed unable to lead the day's conversation

We began to fight about it in the tiny waiting room instead

"Don't ever ask me that again," I said when my husband asked me if I had anything I wanted to talk about. "I won't ever have anything again," I told him

So he brought up something from six years earlier, an incident I had long since forgotten about; something about how I had set up a double date with another couple, then said I was sick and not gone

"If *I* had been sick, she would have cancelled," Lee said. "But because it was her, she made me go"

It felt like my husband was tattling on me to Dr. X

It also felt like all my husband had had to do in that situation was to tell me no

I had said early on in our therapy that one of my concerns was feeling too dominant; that I wanted Lee to make more decisions, to lead us more

I don't remember what Dr. X said, what more Lee said

I was staring out the window from my periphery, counting the tassels on the rug under my feet

Afterward, we rode the elevator down to the basement to use the bathroom and discuss the day's conversation, as was our habit

"I feel like I'm going to throw up," my husband said

"We don't have to go back," I said

I wondered if I was being dominant again in making this suggestion

"Or we could take a week off," I said

We were paying a lot of money to tread water, to discuss minor events from six years before

We walked down the street to a bar we hadn't been to in a decade

It was Happy Hour and we each ordered a drink at the bar

"I feel better already," my husband said

"See," I said.

"A week off would be good," he said

"Exactly," I said

I was studying the appetizers; I was always famished after therapy

"Let's cheers," my husband said

The bartender had just brought us our drinks

I held mine in the air

"To the end of couples therapy," my husband said

"To the end," I said

We clinked glasses and I took a sip of mine while my husband emptied his

"I think we did pretty well," he said

"Very well," I agreed

"Astonishingly well!"

"Fantastically well!"

I was hoping this meant we never had to go back

The amount and type of problems we had now seemed reasonable

We weren't going to fix any more problems that year, at least

There was a limit and we had reached ours

"Let's go somewhere that has Keno," my husband said

"There's only that one burger place in that one strip mall," I said

"Yes," my husband said. "Let's go there!"

"Okay," I said

We hadn't played Keno in a long time. We sat in a back booth and ate cheeseburgers and picked numbers and watched for the numbers on a large television screen on the wall

"This is much better than therapy," I said

"Much, much better," Lee said

"Two of my numbers just came up!" I said

I was watching the TV screen overhead

I was wiping barbeque sauce from my chin

My Old Man

My ex (husband) was in a bad way
In the voicemail he left me he said my name three times
I had his number listed in my phone under "Dad"
"Hold on," I would say to whoever was in the room.
"Dad is calling."

It was never good news when Dad called
He was the only person in my life who still called me Beth.

He'd been manic all summer
Ever since he'd moved back from Ohio.
His mother had given him twenty thousand dollars cash as payment for the manufactured house I'd bought him the year before.
Now his sister was living in it with her six cats.

"I can't fucking live in a trailer with my sister and six cats," he'd said.

I agreed, but I thought it was shitty of his mother and sister to stiff him on the other twenty thousand.

"I couldn't stay another day in Ohio," he said.

It didn't take him long to blow through the twenty grand. The next time we saw him he had an old American beater, a Chevy or Ford four-door, and a run down apartment in the town where we lived when our daughter was a baby.

We sat, my daughter and I, on straight back kitchen chairs in the living room and he sat on a cot covered in a sleeping bag.

The two bedrooms were empty. There was a cat litter pan in the kitchen.

"I bought a piece of land up north near where Grandma and Grandpa used to live, remember?" he said.

"I remember," I said—our daughter was too young to remember

"I bought a piece of land and an old camper and when my lease runs out at the end of summer, I'll move up and live in the camper."

That was four months ago, when he told us about the land he'd bought.

Now it was nearing the middle of September. When he left me the voicemail, there were two days until his lease was up.

"I don't know what I'm going to do, Beth," he said in the voicemail. "I can't live in the camper. There isn't any plumbing. There isn't any heat or electricity. I'll have to ride my bike into town to take a shit."

I listened to the voicemail once and deleted it. I couldn't bear to listen to it a second time. I kept hearing his words, "I don't know if you can help me, Beth. I'm kind of out of options."

I mailed his sister a postcard. We hadn't spoken in fourteen years. I wrote my number on the postcard, asked her to call me.

Three days later I had a text message from his sister on my phone. I took a deep breath and dialed her number. I listened to her tell me why she and her mother had washed their hands of my ex. I listened to her talk for an hour.

It was no use yelling. I didn't bother adding her number into my phone.

He had a father also but his father was living in a van outside a series of motel rooms. "He rents the motel rooms for the wifi but he can't sleep in the beds cuz of his back. He sleeps in a reclining chair in the back of his van," my ex had told my daughter and me earlier in the summer

My daughter and my stepdaughter and I were my ex's only family. It was a lot of responsibility. He was drinking again and smoking weed again and now he was taking Klonopin, also.

"He doesn't remember sometimes when I call," my daughter said. "He said he didn't remember me visiting him two weeks ago."

I pictured my daughter's father as one of the men I passed downtown on the street. He'd lived at the YMCA a decade earlier. He'd lived above a guy known as Shaky Jake in an assisted living apartment after that. He'd lived in a house I bought him for ten years. It was the longest he'd ever lived anywhere. Until he moved to live near his mom in Ohio.

He was forty years old and he'd been working odd jobs since he'd dropped out of school at fifteen. He'd worked as a house painter and a maintenance man and a bar cook and a dishwasher. He'd worked as a dishwasher in eight to twelve different establishments. He said, "I'm never washing another dish as long as I live." He said, "I'd rather eat out of a dumpster than ever wash another dish again."

I called my mom. She'd recently moved back from Florida after the death of her fourth husband. We hadn't been talking and now we were again. I called her because my ex liked her. I called her because they'd always gotten along, even though she and I often didn't.

We called my ex and my daughter and my stepdaughter, arranged to meet that Sunday at one pm.

It wasn't what you call an intervention because none of us had written anything down. My current husband had spent three hours making phone calls to various organizations and mental health facilities around town.

We met at a Burger King in the town where my ex and I had lived with my daughter until I left him when she was six. We'd lived in that town another two years, my daughter and I, in an apartment across from the Kmart.

We bought five cups for soda and sat at a table in the middle of the Burger King. It was two o'clock on a Sunday. There was a woman seated alone at a table beside us. She had a small container of onions and was dipping them in a glob of ketchup.

My ex said, "This isn't how I thought my life would turn out."
He said, "This isn't anyone's fault."
I looked up and he was looking at me.
I hadn't thought it was my fault.
He hadn't dated anyone in the fourteen years since our divorce.

He was wearing a ten year old pair of jeans, a t shirt and a flannel.
He was wearing an old ball cap on account of the tattoo he'd gotten on his forehead when I was pregnant with our daughter. It was a blue star and he'd tried several times to have it removed, first with a laser and then with a knife. Nothing worked.

My mother said, "Oh, honey. You just need a shower and to get yourself cleaned up."

My ex said, "They're legalizing euthanasia in Oregon."
He said, "I don't have much longer on this earth."
He said, "I don't want to be a burden to anyone."

I said, "Don't talk like that. You're not a burden."
I said, "You just need to stop drinking so you can think straight."

His two daughters weren't saying anything. One was across from me. The other was beside me. He was fifteen and twenty when they were born. He couldn't even buy alcohol. They both had their heads down.

He said he was staying at a Knights Inn a town over. I handed him the pages of AA meetings I'd printed out for him. I'd highlighted the ones in the town in which we'd raised our daughter.

"I haven't been to an AA meeting in ten years," he said, looking at the papers.

"There's one tonight at eight at the church on Anne Street and one tomorrow morning at nine thirty at the church by the pond where we used to feed ducks," I said.

I knew my daughter was thinking about "white duck" now. There'd been about twenty regular colored ducks and one white one when we used to go, the three of us, to feed them when she was little, walked from the old farmhouse in which we lived down to the park by the pond.

My ex hadn't been drinking then. Or if he was, I wasn't aware of it.

"I've got a hose I can run up the exhaust into the camper," my ex was saying. "Be a lot easier for everyone."

"No," I said. "You're not doing that. Don't talk like that in front of the girls"

"Come on, honey," my mom said. Her hand was patting his leg. The girls didn't look up.

"We're going to find a rehab place," I said. "We're going to find a place tomorrow."

"You just need to take a shower and get some sleep," my mom said. Her hand was still on his leg and I was grateful for it. It'd been fourteen years, maybe fifteen, since my hand was there.

"Am I that dirty?" he said. "Do I smell?"

I glanced at his fingernails. They were a little dirty.

"No," I said. He didn't smell.

When we stood to leave, the woman who had been eating onions stood and said something to my ex. She was in her fifties and chubby and had a perm. I heard her say, "I couldn't help overhearing," and then I didn't hear what else she said.

Outside on the sidewalk my ex said, "She invited me to her church."

"That was nice," I said.

The girls hugged their father and my mother hugged their father and I stood by myself by the car. I hadn't hugged him in fourteen years.

"I'll call you in the morning," I said.

"Get some sleep, honey," my mother said.

That night we went to get Chinese with my husband. We played a word game and went to bed. I didn't think of my ex in his bed at the Knights Inn. I didn't think of whether he'd showered or not, whether or not he'd gone to AA.

In the morning my husband went to his job at the university and my mother and I started dialing numbers.

A few days earlier I had asked different friends and family members what I should do. A couple people had suggested I go to Al-Anon. I didn't think they understood the situation. My ex was ill. It was like suggesting someone who wants to help a person with Down syndrome is codependent. No one would question your instinct to help a person with Down syndrome.

I didn't know why I always seemed to ask other people for advice. Maybe that instinct was part of my codependency.

We weren't getting anywhere with dialing numbers. We got in the car and drove to a building, talked to a woman. She gave us more numbers to dial. We went home and talked to more people on the telephone.

Finally there was a person who could take him, a rehab place just over the state line in Ohio. My ex hated Ohio but I tried not to think about that.

He drove down and we took two cars to Ohio. I asked my mother to take my ex because I didn't like being alone in a car with him. I didn't mind being in a car with him with my daughter but I didn't like being alone with him. I would start thinking about how he'd never dated anyone after our divorce. I would start thinking about how he'd told our daughter he sometimes thought about how his wife was married to someone else now.

I didn't feel comfortable alone with my ex.

My mother was going to drive back to her place in Ohio once they admitted my ex into rehab.

We never thought, *What if they won't admit him.*

The woman my mother had talked to on the phone had sounded so confident.

We sat in the waiting room, which was smaller than your average waiting room. There were no accessible restrooms and a TV was playing *Gunsmoke*. My mother sat beside my ex and helped him fill out paperwork.

She said, "Do you feel like harming yourself or others?"

"That's an impossible question to answer," my ex said.

"Do you feel like harming yourself *right now*," my mom said. "Are you suicidal *right now*?"

She kept emphasizing *right now*.

It reminded me of the scene in *Harold & Maude* in which the mother answers the dating questionnaire for Harold.

My mother checked, "No" a bunch of times.

People were starting to trickle in. Mostly young men and women in their twenties. They wrote their names on nametags and stuck the nametags to their chests. I avoided their chests, avoided learning their names.

It was starting to feel overwhelming sitting in the waiting room, like too much oxygen was in use. It felt overwhelming that you had to ask to use a bathroom; that someone had to take you.

Suddenly the doors swung open and all the people with nametags went behind them. Only one woman with a baby stayed behind.

"They won't let me go back," she said to one of the women behind the counter. "Because of her," she said and pointed to the baby.

The baby was on the floor in a plastic baby carrier. We all looked at the baby.

"She's two weeks old," the woman with the nametag said. "She was born addicted so she's small. She keeps losing weight."

The baby started fussing and the woman got out a bottle and propped it in the baby's hands. The baby's hands were tiny. The bottle kept sliding around.

"Her father doesn't have the parental instinct like I do," the woman was saying. "I can't trust him."

The bottle kept sliding around and the baby kept crying. It was uncomfortable sitting in the waiting room. It still felt like there wasn't enough oxygen.

"I'll tell them exactly what's in my bloodstream," my ex said.

"At least you're honest," the mother of the baby said.

I don't know why but I kept thinking of the movie, *Trainspotting*. I'd breastfed my daughter exclusively. It was hard for me to be around crying babies. I wanted to nurse all of them like Salma Hayek had nursed that one baby in an orphanage or wherever.

The door opened and a woman called, "Jared?" My ex stood.

"Good luck, Jared," the mother of the baby said.

"I have to get some air," I said after Jared had gone back.

It was a beautiful autumn day outside, eighty degrees and sunny. I lay down on a picnic table bench, my hair touching the grass beneath me.

I sent a text to my mother who was still inside, "What if they don't take him."

"Think positive," my mother texted back.

I lay on the picnic bench twenty minutes, trying to think positive. My mother hadn't gone without a drink, to my knowledge, in thirty-five years. But she was functioning. She wasn't living in a camper with no electricity, no plumbing. She didn't have to ride her bike into town to take a shit.

My mother was on the sidewalk outside the facility.

"Come on," she said. "They're calling us back."

I'd been in similar situations with my ex in the past. Twice he'd been admitted to hospitals. Each of those times we'd taken him to the ER. A third time they hadn't admitted him and I'd had to drive home with him, him knowing I'd tried to admit him, tried to rid myself of the burden of him. I'd gotten a motel room with our daughter that time. A few months later I'd gotten a divorce. I'd thought I'd rid myself of the burden of him, even though a week after the divorce I was driving him to a doctor's appointment, same as always.

We walked past the mother of the baby, through the doors to the back. We were shown into a room, took seats on other side of my ex.

A young woman, not much older than our daughter, sat smiling in a chair across from us. Her smile was dumb but I didn't yet hate her.

"We're not going to admit him," she said. "He hasn't had alcohol in three days."

He hadn't had alcohol in three days because we'd told him not to drink. My mother had checked "no" under suicidal because she'd asked him if he wanted to kill himself *right now*. These were two of the ways we had fucked up.

"What about the Klonopin?" I said.

"He says he has a prescription," the young woman said.

"But what if he doesn't?" I said. I didn't think he had a prescription even though he kept insisting to our daughter and everyone he had a prescription.

The young woman shrugged and smiled.

"What are we supposed to do now?" I said. "What if he's homeless?" I said.

The young woman said my ex qualified for out patient treatment. I didn't understand how he was going to get himself to a daily out patient treatment facility when he didn't have a place of residence, when the only place he had to live was in a camper two hours from anything.

I hated the young woman for making me ask these questions in front of my ex. I hated the young woman for being the decider of our fates. I thought there had to be a mistake. I thought surely an older man had to make that sort of decision. Someone with more thoughts in his head. (This is an example of a Democrat being sexist.)

"I have to use the bathroom," I said. I took as long as I could going to the bathroom. I didn't want to drive the hour back alone with my ex. I had his nail clippers and his incense and his lighter in my purse.

My ex and my mother were waiting on the sidewalk for me. It was still sunny and I just wanted to lie down again. My mother and my ex were smoking. My mother said, "What do you want to do?" I was yelling but I can't remember what I said. I knew my ex would think I was angry with him even though I was angry with everyone else. I was angry that I was in charge. I had gotten a divorce so I wouldn't have to make any more decisions.

"Do you want me to drive him back?" my mother said.

I nodded even though I knew nodding was a horrible thing to do in this situation. I knew I was being selfish. I was a horrible person because I felt nauseous at the thought of being alone in the car for an hour with my ex.

I had gotten a divorce because I hadn't wanted to be alone with him anymore.

I studied my mother and my ex in my rearview mirror. I called my husband to complain. I texted my daughter while driving.

WHAT ARE YOU GOING TO DO NOW? I kept thinking.
I didn't know WHAT I WAS GOING TO DO NOW.
I wanted someone else to tell me WHAT TO DO.
I didn't want to have to make any more decisions.

When we got back to the house my husband was there.
My ex came inside, "Can I have my keys?"
I'd hung the keys to his car on our key rack when I thought he was going to be away awhile.
I went and got his keys.
I gave him back his nail clippers and incense and lighter.
I gave him the numbers of the places I'd written down in town.
I told him to call the numbers. I told him we'd keep trying.
I told him not to do anything stupid, to think of the girls.

"I just want to get back up to my camp tonight," he said.

My mother said, "I just want to get home."

After my ex left I felt sick.
I was still worried he thought I was angry with him.
He'd told my mother on the drive back, "This isn't Beth's fault."
I dialed his number. I was surprised he answered.

"I wasn't angry with you," I said. "I was angry with that woman, I was angry with everything else."

"I didn't think you were angry with me," he said.

"I just want to get to my camp," he said.

"Okay," I said. "I'll call you tomorrow," I said.

We felt like failures, my mother and I.

"He took back the bullets," my mother said. "The bullets he gave me when he thought he was going to rehab."

I didn't hear from him the next day and I didn't call him either. I was tired. I needed a reprieve.

The day after that he called to say he'd gone to one of the places we'd called. He was on a waiting list for a bed, he said. It could be a few days or a few weeks. It was hard for them to predict, he said.

He sounded upbeat. He sounded okay. I threw away the pages of numbers I'd written in a notebook. I went about my life again. My daughter called her father every Sunday again. He was living in the camper up north but he was calling the place with the bed. He was on a waiting list.

Ginger and Pink

Were the names we had decided on, back in '94 when we met.
It was the spring Kurt Cobain shot himself.
It was the June O.J. killed Nicole.
We met in April, the day before my twenty-fifth birthday,
By mid-May we were married, three months before he turned nineteen.

We were going to change our names legally to Ginger and Pink Quest.
We'd taken acid the night he proposed.
He had a friend, Matt Quest.
He'd always been envious that surname.

But it cost five hundred dollars to change your name.
You had to go before a judge.
It didn't take much to get married.
I wore a skirt from The Gap.

We had to go before a judge in Flint, Michigan to get divorced.
We used my lawyer.
I picked him up from his apartment, drove us to the courthouse.
I had just turned thirty-three. He was six years younger.
Our daughter was six.
He was the same age Kurt was when he shot himself.

I hadn't done acid since the night he proposed.
Hadn't watched *The Wall* again either.

My Old Man II

Four weeks later I had another voicemail from my ex. It was a Sunday afternoon in
October. My husband was in the other room, getting papers ready to take back to
his apartment. We spent weekends together at the house. Weekdays he went to his
apartment—went to his office on campus.

At the start of the message my ex didn't sound so abnormal. He said, "I was hoping I'd
never have to bother you again."
After that, the message quickly devolved to him shouting.
I held the phone away from my ear
I was thinking about a time he'd ripped his hair from his head when he thought I was
cheating on him.
I'd written about it. It sounded romantic on the page.
I was so removed from that night by then
(ten years removed)
(I'd forgotten what it was like to be screamed at in such short distance/close proximity)

(I remembered scooting across the floor of our one bedroom apartment toward the door;
sitting with my back to it for hours, *just in case*)

(I remembered a motel on the same street as our apartment, going there 'on occasion,'
knowing no one to call)

I held the phone close again
He said, "THEY DIDN'T LET ME HAVE MY MEDICATIONS!"
He said, "THEY DIDN'T FEED ME FOR THREE FUCKING DAYS!"
He said, "NEXT TIME THE PIGS BETTER BE PREPARED TO DIE FOR THEIR COUNTRY!"
He said, "AGGGGGGGGGGGHHHHHHHH!"

I waited an hour and dialed his number.
I felt my stomach grow ten times heavier.
I thought maybe I'd forgotten swallowing the pits of ten thousand cherries.

I was remembering driving him to the ER the time he drunkenly got in a fight with my
ex-fiance
He'd returned to our apartment barefooted, his shoulder dislocated, his Jim Morrison hair
ratted and curtaining his face
He moaned and yelled all the way to the hospital
It was my first time driving the van we would later take ross country, after first selling or
giving away all our possessions

"Where are you now?" I asked when he answered.

"I'm back at the camper," he said. "I had to give them all my money and all the money on my credit card to get my car back."

He said, "THEY TOOK MY FUCKING MEDICINE. I HAVEN'T SLEPT IN THREE FUCKING DAYS!"

I found myself standing in my bathroom, absently walking.
I was at a dead end.
I was saying things like, "calm down" and "you just need to get some sleep"
I was trying to sound unaffected but tears were streaming down my face

He said, "AGGGGGGGGGGGHHHHHHHH!"

I kept walking and my stomach was consumed with fire

I heard myself repeating words I'd already said.
I said, "I'll call you in the morning" and "we'll figure something out then."

He said, "THIS ISN'T YOUR PROBLEM."
He said, "I SHOULDN'T HAVE CALLED YOU."

I said, "Think of the girls" and "we're family."

He hung up and I kept walking around the house.
I didn't know where I was going.
I couldn't remember what I was doing before he called.

I found his mother's number.
I hadn't talked to her in sixteen years.
My stomach felt hard and hot.
She answered; it turned out he had called her, too.
But he'd hung up sooner. He told her he'd been kidnapped and then "click."
Or that was her version.
He'd had a nanny as a child, an old lady who lived with him and his mom and his sister.
His mom had worked nights in the ER, slept off her days (with the aid of prescription drugs, he said).
Now she was married to a (retired) cop (he said).

She said, "I don't know what to believe."
She said, "He manipulates."

I said, "Well now your daughter lives in the house I bought for him and he's homeless, so thanks for that," and I hung up.

I threw my phone because I could not slam it down into a receiver as you could in my youth.

I threw my phone because she was not going to be the person I wanted her to be.

It was like starting from scratch every time.

Looking up numbers on the internet.

Trying to figure out the system.

We didn't know his exact location
He'd told our daughter, "GPS would be of no use to you up here"
I pictured a scene out of *Into the Wild*
I remembered a newspaper clipping I'd read two summers before about a man's son who suffered from bipolar disorder dying in a jail cell—
from lack of water (they said)

the father's guilt, of letting his son go to jail rather than rescuing him

I heard the words of my ex's mother "Maybe the best thing for him would be to get picked up by the cops"

But he already had been picked up by the cops and nothing good had happened

They'd turned him out worse than before.

Now he was worse than before.

My Old Man III

I get dressed, drive with the windows down, the radio tuned to the country station
I walk through the grocery store with my boiling gut
Concentrate on not being sick in the frozen food aisle
Buy Eggo waffles

I feel sick all day now

I turn off my phone
Open the book about Dylan
Go upstairs to write
Watch another documentary about Dylan

I have my own mythology
But what is that worth
At a time like this

Xmas Eve Interlude, 1994

I remember he wrapped my present—something inexpensive and rectangular, a CD,
    maybe—in a *Rolling Stone* article about Courtney Love

I remember Courtney Love's face on the outside of my Xmas present,
In December of '94

I don't remember what was inside

We had two cats—Colette and Zelda
And lived in a one bedroom apartment between Twelve and Thirteen Mile Roads in Detroit

This was our first Xmas as husband and wife

A year and a half later I would birth our daughter in a hospital in Flint
Where we'd move to escape his father who had a collection of guns under his bed and
    used his son's social security number to obtain credit cards and phone bills

I don't remember what I got him for Xmas;
Maybe an R. Crumb book.

My Old Man IV

I got another call from my ex
He said, "I'm going to attempt to drive down tomorrow so if you don't hear from me, they got me again."

He said, "I know they put a GPS tracker on my car. I know they bugged my camper. I'm gonna have to get rid of my car and phone soon, too."

It was a voicemail so I didn't have to say 'okay.'

I was eating my Eggo waffles.

I'd been trying not to think about my ex but not thinking about my ex was impossible because he was my daughter's father.

When I checked my phone the next morning there was a voicemail but it wasn't my ex. It was a man my ex had painted houses with off and on the last ten years. *Gordie.*

"I don't know what I just witnessed but I'm concerned," the voice on my phone—Gordie—was saying.

"I asked Jared for your number because I'd heard him talk about you over the years," the voice—Gordie—said.

I dialed my ex but his phone was off and he hadn't made it so you could leave a voicemail.

It was my (current) husband's day off work and we had plans for the day but now my husband was calling Gordie.

I said, "Watch my phone in case Jared calls." I had to shower.

Of course Jared called while I was in the shower!

He didn't seem to mind that my husband had answered my phone.

He talked to him as if he was talking to me. (The audience was the least important part.)

An hour later we met him in a park downtown. I was in the front seat with my current husband. I dialed my ex's number.

"Yes, dear?" he said. He hadn't called me "dear" since the divorce. I tried not to stop and think about it.

"We're parked in front of the basketball court," I said.

"Oh, you dumbasses," he said. "I'm parked right next to you."

We turned to look and he was getting out of his car. It was raining and we motioned to the backseat.

"I probably stink," he said, closing the car door. "I haven't showered in days," he said.

"All I smell is cigarette smoke," I said. Same as always.

"I just wanted to give you this painting by an adolescent girl," he said. He handed me a pastel painting with a triangle in the middle of it. Illuminati shit. My daughter's sister's art. "There's a letter taped to the back," he said.

I think he may have said, "love letter" or "goodbye letter." I'm hoping he didn't, though. I'm hoping my memory is faulty. I haven't opened the letter. I don't ever really want to open the letter.

My husband tried to ask him some sort of reasonable question. He had no experience with my ex when he was like this.

My ex's answers had religious overtones. Same as always.

My husband asked if he was at the homeless shelter, if he'd met with a doctor, if he had a plan.

My ex said, "I checked in, I checked out. They're always watching. They're watching us now. God's son is always roaming. I'm seeing a psychiatrist in a couple hours. I scared Gordie, too. I shouldn't have told him the thing about the computer. That was my mistake. I knew it'd freak him out."

"I bought a gun from a pawn shop but I buried it," he said.

"I sold the camper to my neighbor for five hundred dollars. But some of that money might be on the highway," he said.

"Oh, you did that last time, too," I said. I was remembering the first time he was hospitalized, the night before his father taking him for a drive, our rent money flying out the window onto the freeway.

"Well let me ask you this, is it five hundred dollars or twenty-five sheets of paper?" my ex asked us.

"Twenty-five sheets of paper," I said. "I know," I said.

He had trailed off into speaking in tongues or in speaking in what he thought speaking in tongues sounded like. He was motioning a lot with his hands. It reminded me of an actor in a movie. I couldn't remember which one.

"I want you to call me every day," I said.

"Is it okay if I call your wife?" he said, turning toward my husband. He laughed instead of waiting for an answer.

"You're so stupid," he said, turning toward me. "You think . . . never mind."

"Here, take my I.D.," he said, and he pulled his wallet from his pocket.

"I don't want your I.D.," I said. "You're going to need it."

"No, here," he said. He pulled something from his wallet and handed it out to me. It was a joker from a deck of cards. I was stupid.

"Oh," I said. "I remember this trick." It was true; I remembered once before him signing the joker card and handing it to me, before or during one of his hospitalizations.

He laughed and I noticed the hat he was wearing had a light taped to the top of it. I noticed his beard was fuller than I'd ever seen it and there were patches of white. He looked like he'd lost twenty pounds since I'd seen him five weeks earlier.

His sister, when I'd called her then to try to get her to help, had said, "He's still quite fat," as though any "extra" weight was evidence of emotional wellbeing.

He was easily definable as "gaunt" now. Sunken cheekbones. Sunken eyes. He was wearing a pair of jeans I'd bought him sixteen years ago. An old pair of moccasins. An old T-shirt and jacket.

My husband and I had met with my ex intending to take him to a hospital. But I could tell neither of us was up for that now. It seemed too great a struggle.

"Do you want us to go with you to the shelter?" I said. "To your appointment?"

"No, no," he said. "I'm good. I ate an orange today. You can sleep there but you have to be out during the day. You have to sign out. I'm just going to park here for four hours, then move the car and park on the other side of the street."

"Okay," I said. "Well, I guess we should get going," I said.

It's hard to convey on the page how our presence seemed to be aggravating him, how his hands were waving about the car, the words coming more rapidly every minute he remained with us.

I sound hysterical on the page whenever I write about him. I haven't figured out a way to write about this without me sounding like an asshole.

I was holding it together while my ex was in the car.

On the drive home I broke down in sobs. I called my mother, sobbing.

My husband and I had tickets for an event that night we no longer felt like attending. We ended up in a back booth at Denny's, instead.

"What was that Brad Pitt movie?" I asked my husband.

"I don't know. There are a lot of Brad Pitt movies, you're going to have to be more specific."

"Think of the context of our previous conversation," I said. I was a dick like that.

"Oh," he said. "*12 Monkeys*?"

"Yeah. That one." Brad Pitt in 12 Monkeys came close to emulating my ex when my ex was like this. But an actor on the screen cannot convey

"I walked out of *A Beautiful Mind*," I said. "It was too realistic," I said. "Also it had some bullshit happy ending."

"I remember you telling me that," my husband said. "Also *The Aviator*," he said.

"I walked out of *The Aviator*?" I said. "I don't remember that."

"Yes," my husband said. "His behavior was too reminiscent you said."

The first movie I remember watching in which a character "goes crazy"—is taken to a mental hospital—was *Frances*. My mother made me watch it with her. Though Frances wasn't supposed to be crazy. That was supposed to be what was so sad about it.

But it's sad even if a person is crazy.

Betty Blue was the second movie. Betty Blue poked her own eye out. I was twenty when I saw *Betty Blue* and Betty was around twenty when she poked her eye out in the movie and the movie was based on a real woman. I worried for a long time after that that I'd do something like that, poke out my eye or 'go crazy.' I didn't leave my apartment for weeks. I sat in a clawed bathtub telling myself not to think about going crazy. I had panic attacks at night.

This was four years before I met my ex.

After I met my ex and we got married and had our daughter I came to the agreement with myself that only one parent could be crazy and since her father was, I couldn't be. I made an agreement with myself to hold myself together.

My Old Man V

I was terrified and I was ashamed to be terrified.
But I went around anyway, locking all the windows and doors.
I bolted the door to the garage, which I had never before bolted.
I slid the sticks in the sliding glass doors upstairs and down which I had never done before.

Previously my ex had locked all the windows when he house and dog sat for us a decade
    earlier.

"God," I'd said to my husband when we returned. "He's even locked the windows." I went
    around unlocking each window and opening them to let in fresh air.

Earlier in the day my ex's caseworker had told us he'd checked out of the shelter.

"What reason did he give?" my husband had asked.

"He said he couldn't sleep."

No shit he couldn't sleep. He was manic and out of Klonopin.

I imagined him driving down our street at two a.m.

Our house was mostly windows, mostly glass.

It had never bothered me before.

Now I felt like a woman in a horror movie or a Stephen King novel,
Like I was being watched.

I kept stopping to look out the front window. We lived on a dirt road with no streetlights.
    Everything that had never bothered me before suddenly bothered me.

Suddenly the freedom I'd wanted and asked for felt like a dumb idea.

The nights my husband stayed at his apartment I hid in my bedroom, locked my bedroom
    door, listened for the sound of a car.

"Can I just park at the end of your driveway and sleep in my car?" my ex had asked a
    month earlier.

"No," I'd said. "Absolutely not," I'd said.

128

He was calling every day to check in, leaving me a voicemail with the date and time.

I had to keep reminding myself he had called me five weeks earlier, he had asked or begged me for help.

I sat in my office upstairs watching *Alice*, an old TV sitcom from the '70s because it took my mind momentarily off my ex.

I was starting to feel like I was going a little crazy.

I couldn't stop thinking, I was having a hard time sleeping, I was waking up in the middle of the night unable to get back to sleep.

My Old Man VI

My daughter came home from college for the weekend.
I was standing at the door by the garage when she walked in.

"What's going on?" she said. "You're never this happy to see me."

I didn't typically hug her when she arrived.

It was October and I'd made her favorite Halloween cupcakes.

After she ate one I told her I wanted to talk with her and her sister.

She set the computer up on the kitchen table and we sat on chairs in front of it.

Her sister was on Facetime on the computer. I knew she was sitting on her bed because I recognized the tie-dye fabric on the wall behind her.

I told them everything that had happened with their father in the last week.
I told them the ways we were trying to get him help.

I knew it was frustrating for them as well. They'd been there a month earlier when he was asking for help. The three of us believed he still wanted help even if his mania had moved him past the point of asking and the laws were preventing us from getting him any.

"It's like, if you saw a woman unconscious and bleeding in the street, you wouldn't wait for her to come to consciousness before taking her to a hospital. No one would be like, 'Well, maybe she doesn't want help. Maybe she wants her freedom lying here in this street, bleeding.'"

"Right. I know."

We were having a bonfire that night. We had invited my daughter's sister but at the last minute she was called into work and couldn't go.

One of my daughter's friends had just returned from L.A. and I asked her about it as we stood around the fire.

"I was attacked on Venice Beach," she said. "I don't know why this kind of stuff always happens to me. It was a woman *without a permanent residence*. I was waiting in line to use a bathroom and she said, 'Go back to Puerto Rico.' And, 'Make sure you wipe your pussy.' I was hoping she'd be gone when I came out of the bathroom but she was right there waiting on me. She was schizophrenic or something. She said to me, 'Did you wipe your pussy?' and I told her to stay away from me and she threw whatever was in her bottle at me. I didn't know if it was water or something else."

And then someone else, another of my daughter's friends said, "Yeah, I didn't know there were so many homeless people in California until I went to San Francisco."

And someone else said, "I don't fuck with the homeless people in Ann Arbor anymore. They're mean now."

I pictured my daughter's father as one of the homeless men walking around downtown, sitting in the park, talking to passersby.

I felt like the one audience member at a comedy show who says, "That's not funny, my ___ is ___."

But no one had made a joke and I hated those people anyhow.

My Ex Part X

I was waiting on a call from my ex's caseworker

For the second time in two months, my ex had agreed to voluntarily enter a rehab hospital in Ohio, the same rehab hospital my mother and I had driven him to seven weeks before

This time his caseworker was driving him

It was Halloween and I was feeling homesick for our daughter

My ex had been homeless two weeks

He'd been living in a camp in upstate Michigan for a month before that

I couldn't remember how long it'd been since he'd given away his cats

We'd owned at least one cat since I'd met him and I'd met him twenty-three years ago

I wondered how long it'd be before he was stable enough again to own a cat

We'd camped across America in the fall of '94, three months after we'd married

In Minnesota we'd stayed in a campground high on a hill

It was September and we were the only ones there

My ex is shirtless in the photographs from that campsite

A stray cat is on his lap; he is seated in a camp chair by the fire

His hair is long and jet black and wavy

The celebrity I always compare him to is Jim Morrison

I can't remember what sex with him felt like but I remember we had sex every night for a year

Us and Them – Halloween evening, 2016

I went for a walk as a way of dealing with my anxieties
Waiting to hear if the rehab hospital in Ohio would take my ex was like waiting to hear about finding a liver match

I didn't know what we were going to do if they didn't take him this time

In the past week he'd left me seven voicemails, half of them at four in the morning, Most of them riddles; I forget the questions but the answer to one was, "Because Santa Claus only cums once a year"

I had seen earlier in the day that Roger Waters was on Marc Maron

I leashed my dog and got out my iPod

It was four thirty and trick-or-treat started at five and I didn't want to be home when it started

I made a sign that said "take one, please" and taped it to a plastic pumpkin filled with "fun size" candy bars

I didn't like trick-or-treat now that my daughter was away at college and now that trick-or-treat started before dusk

When we were newly married and camping across the country, my ex and I had listened to three rock and roll bands: Led Zeppelin, The Grateful Dead and Pink Floyd

My ex didn't like TV or movies or books

My ex was born thirty years too late

I was eager to hear Roger Waters talk about Pink Floyd

I was especially interested in hearing him talk about Syd Barrett since Syd Barrett had ended up in a mental hospital and then living the rest of his life with his mother

I wanted to know how Roger Waters had met Syd Barrett and about Syd Barrett's contribution to the band

But Roger Waters didn't want to talk about Pink Floyd

Roger Waters wanted us to care about his solo career while still naming his tour after a song from his previous band

Roger Waters wanted to talk about all the poor people he played music for in Mexico and the U.S.

He said, "Everywhere I go with *The Wall*, whenever we do 'Brick II' anywhere, I always have local children to come and sing and I always try to get them from the most disadvantaged background that I can find. Anyway, we did a gig in San Diego a few years ago and I looked at these kids and I thought, 'These aren't my kids. I don't know who they are but . . . ' So anyway, I found out that they were the children of the executives from the arena who thought it'd be fun for their kids to be part of the show. So I went ape-shit and got rid of them all. 'Find me some proper kids!' So these kids turned up and I went, 'These are more like it. These are my kids. This is my constituency.'"

I hated when old rock celebrities tried to convince you of how humanitarian they were while living in mansions and sending their own kids to private schools.

I wanted Marc to ask Roger about how he'd raised his own kids, about how his own kids were less "my constituency" than the arena executives' kids, but Marc didn't ask anything about that.

I remembered how my friend who is a teacher at a small, expensive private school in L.A. had Roger Waters' grandchild in her class the previous year, how the mother of the child had invited my friend to stay at the family castle if she was ever in England.

I thought Roger Waters was full of shit, I mean

I thought more often than not, it was better when a rock and roll figure died at a young age, before they became bloated and self-important and boring.

I was glad Kurt wasn't alive to disavow Nirvana or his band members or to talk about how selfish other people were while living the life of a bloated multi-millionaire

I was halfway home when a man in a parked car on a cul-de-sac rolled down his window and said something to me

I took out my earbud and said, "What?"

He said, "There's a buck over there."

I looked in the direction the man was pointing but I didn't see anything
I took a step forward and looked again and on the side of the house was a tall, male deer, just like the man had said

I nodded and waved and kept walking

All around me people were readying their house for trick-or-treat and I was trying not to think about what would happen to my daughter's father if the rehab hospital didn't take him

I left the "take one, please" sign on the plastic pumpkin on my porch and went inside

I didn't feel like answering my door or saying "Happy Halloween"

I didn't know why people said that mental illness was the same as any other illness and then treated it and the people suffering from it differently

(my ex's mother, for instance, had called him "manipulative")

I didn't know if I was more concerned about my ex husband being homeless or about my daughter having a homeless father

A little of both, I guessed

Us and them

'DAD'

I was in the basement storage room scooping the cat litter

It was almost Thanksgiving

There was cat litter all over the floor

There was a lone turd on the carpet

I reached to pick up the turd, to flick it back into the box

As I bent over my eye was drawn into a cardboard box

There was a small gap where the cardboard flaps did not meet or had come apart

I saw a photo album my daughter had made for her father

For his birthday or Father's Day, I forgot which

The photo album said, "DAD" on the outside cover and under the word DAD was a
    photograph of my daughter and her father

In the photograph my daughter is five years old and standing, proudly, in her father's
    work boots

In the photograph my daughter's hair is in pigtails and her father is almost smiling

The photograph was taken the winter before we left him

In six months she and I would be living in a new apartment complex on the other side of
    town next to the Kmart

In six months he will be living in an upstairs room of his sister's house

I flicked the turd back into the box and left the room

The next time I scooped cat litter I purposefully avoided looking into the cardboard box

Jared pt whatever

I don't look at my phone for two and a half days and when I do I have seven new
 voicemails from my ex

Three are left at four in the morning

I put off listening to them

I ask my husband to listen to them the next time he comes over

I ask my daughter to ask my ex to stop calling me

My ex went before a judge to get out of the hospital a week after he went in

My ex is living in his car, is back on Klonopin

He rear-ends my stepdaughter when he follows her to a restaurant

He tells her, "I'm just in love with this car right now" when she asks him if he needs help
 finding a cheap apartment or mobile home rental

My daughter says, "I just talked to Dad"

My daughter says, "I'm so livid"

She says, "He's back on Klonopin"

"I know," I say

I sigh

It's the first Thanksgiving in twenty-two years I haven't talked to my daughter's father

I am conscious of not reminding her to call him

I don't know if either of us can take any more loss of hope

(unfinished)

ELLIOTT SMITH SONGS

(September, 2014–April, 2015)

I Was Lying in 2009 When I Said I Would Be the One
to Plunge the Knife into Your Heart; I Am Sorry

I am writing you these poems in avoidance of finishing the novel I am writing about us
I am writing you these poems in avoidance of replying to the emails you sent me 7
    weeks ago
I am writing you these poems in avoidance of being the one who stabs you to death at
    your (final) reading

I am sorry about the last thing mostly
I know how much it would mean to you

(Believe me when I say it would mean that much to me also)

(You have already finished more books than you told me you wanted to finish before you
    commit suicide or before I stab you to death and I'm sorry about that also)

I am sorry I am such a coward and also so noncommittal
I can't seem to finish anything
It is unlikely I will finish this poetry collection but it is all I have of you currently

I am not very agile with a knife either.

Not Replying to Your Email Is Making Me Feel Insane

I told myself I was not going to reply to your email
(it was the first time you'd emailed me in four and a half years)
Because I was trying to be a better person
(For someone else, not for you, I am sorry)

It seems inevitable I will not be a better person or a person who
gets better

I wrote a 'Modern Love' essay about not replying to your email
In order to deal with the anxiety I was feeling about not replying to your email

I felt a sense of guilt about using your real name in the Modern Love essay

(the submission page said real names were required)
(when I say 'your real name' I mean the name you publish your writing under not your
actual 'real name')
(but still)

I probably will not let them use my essay if they want it
(because of the feelings of guilt about using your real name)
But they probably won't so whatever

Deleting your blog was a genius move because if you hadn't deleted
Your blog I could have comfortably gone on with my life never
Replying to your email and not even thinking about replying to your email

(which was how things were going!)

After you deleted your blog I realized I had no way of ever feeling
Like I know you're alive without emailing you
and it's hard to deal with the feeling of you not being alive
or not being somewhere on the internet where I can find you
every time I get online
and sometimes multiple times
while I am online.

The night before I wrote the Modern Love essay I opened one of your
recent emails and constructed a reply and stared at my reply for approx. four mins
without sending it

I allowed my computer arrow to hover over the 'send' button in a way that now seems mildly 'dangerous'

Eventually, I deleted the words I had typed to you
And signed out of my email without accidentally sending the email and then put Beyoncé on my iPod and danced around my basement in an effort to unburden myself of the anxiety and false excitement
I was feeling from having almost replied to your email.

in the middle of the night I woke and felt relieved I had not replied to your email
though now another twenty-four hours have passed and I'm still thinking about how I'm not replying to your email
so it seems like I never got over not replying to your email

I cannot say with any semblance of confidence if I will or will not
reply to your email in the next three hundred and sixty five days
but I will probably think about whether or not I will or will not reply
to your email every day of the next three hundred and sixty five
which makes me feel tired in a way
I probably would not feel if I just replied to your email.

Reading Your ask.fm Made Me Feel Like I Was Having a Direct Conversation with You in a Way that Was Satisfying

Before you deleted your ask.fm account
I would read it every night before I went to bed
and it felt like we were having this
very enthusiastic, long-winded conversation about life,
almost like we did five years ago
when we still talked on the phone,
or four and a half years ago,
after we stopped talking on the phone,
but while we were still emailing and texting.

Everything you said on your ask.fm
I took as a direct message to me
in the way Letterman's stalker did
before she killed herself on the train track
and I felt content in a way I hadn't
since we stopped talking

I wondered if that was how Letterman's stalker once felt,
before the incident on the train tracks
but after she became convinced Letterman was sending her messages through her TV

Which isn't to say I'm going to kill myself now or something.

Before She Killed Herself Letterman's Stalker Stalked an Astronaut Also

But the astronaut wasn't famous, or wasn't on TV, or something.

What I mean is, I don't know how Letterman's stalker became convinced the astronaut
was communicating with her

In the absence of TV or ask.fm or the internet or whatever

I Don't Know Where to Find You Now That You're Not on the Internet

I watched a documentary on the photographer
Francesca Woodman tonight
and at the part in which her parents recount her death
(from jumping off a building in NYC)
I felt a great sense of guilt (and brokenness) with regard to you.

There had been mention of a lover who had split from her—

This man: http://www.holstengalleries.com/artists/show/moore-18

I wondered afterward what it must be like to be him,
Alive and doing glasswork in Seattle

If he had a daily awareness of his place in the world
As the cause of this great pain of this now (famously) deceased artist
If he was aware his place on her Wikipedia page.

He was not interviewed in the movie with her parents.

I wondered if I should email you a reply,
To ask if you are okay, if you are well,

I wondered:
When does my loyalty to my husband
Become abandonment of you.
When is trying to be a good person
Turning me into a bad one.

Are you okay?

The Other Night I Watched a Documentary About Harry Dean Stanton (all I do now is watch documentaries alone in my basement)

Harry Dean mostly hummed or sang songs.
He didn't seem to want to talk much.
He told one interesting story
—interesting in how I could relate it back to you and me, I mean—
About a young actress he worked with on *Paris, Texas*.

He was trying to figure out his character's motivation for being mute, he said.
The young actress said she hadn't talked for years as a teen.

"Could you hear what other ppl were saying?" Harry Dean said.

"Yes, I could hear them," she said.

"Then why didn't you talk?" Harry Dean said.

"Because I was afraid what would happen if I opened my mouth, I was afraid I'd start to
    break down," she said.

Maybe I Should Start an ask.fm in Order to Feel Close to You Again

The other night L. and I were cleaning under my daughter's bed for the first time in
    seven years
There were big plastic containers filled with small plastic dinosaurs and the big plastic
    containers were covered with dust.
L. went to get something to dust the plastic containers.
I was holding a large garbage bag and putting loose items into it.
There was a condom wrapper and a Bic lighter and your book.
I was grateful L. wasn't there to see the three items
I was especially glad he wasn't there to see your book.
I think it would be easier for L. to accept the fact that my daughter is smoking weed and
    having sex than to accept the fact that she has read your book.
Before I put your book in the trash bag I flipped through it to make sure it wasn't the copy
    I wrote notes in five years earlier,
even though I knew I had recycled that copy after you didn't take the bus to see me four
    years and nine months ago.

My daughter was the last one of the two of us to speak with you on the phone.

My daughter had your phone number in her phone for six or seven months, maybe more.

The last time you texed her was to ask her to buy me an ice cream at the mall and to say it
    was from you.

I never told you but she never bought me that ice cream.

Which was like you failing me twice. Or three times.
I lost count.

Your Birthday (DOB) Is the Password on My Computer

I'm sorry I never explained to you that I would no longer be replying to your text
    messages or emails.
The last text I remember receiving from you four years ago
Was, "Elizabeth, how are you".
I was in an airport and had just separated myself physically from L.
This was almost exactly a year to the day of the last time I had separated myself physically
    from you.
I have been trying to figure out a way in which a person can effectively combine herself
    with two people at the same time, emotionally, without one or both of the two people
making the person feel like shit.
So far I haven't come up with anything
(even though I have been reading a lot of books about Simone de Beauvoir and Jean-Paul
    Sartre and Henry Miller and Anaïs Nin)

In answer to your question: sometimes I am okay and sometimes I think of you.

No Such Thing As Closure for an Asshole Like Us

This morning my shit smelled sweet
in a way it does
twice a year

And I thought about
how I would be okay
with you walking into the bathroom
this morning,
in a way I wouldn't
be, normally

Which seems
an odd thing to think
about someone
you haven't seen in five years
and likely won't see again
or at least not in the way
that would have them walking into a bathroom
after you shit.

I am trying to remember
what I ate
in the past twenty-four hours
so I can replicate it
in case we ever see each other again
in the way that would have you
following me into a bathroom
after I shit.

Conspiracy Theory

I remember you saying
that titling your poems
was the last thing you did
after you wrote them

I think if you saw the movie *Somewhere*
you would hate it
because you think
movies are a waste of time
but mostly I think about how
no one will talk to me
about you
which feels sometimes like a conspiracy,
against me or against you,
I'm not sure which.

I am staring at the movie poster for *Somewhere* currently.

I think if you were an actor in Hollywood
you would be a lot like Stephen Dorff's character
in that movie

(I know you hate me for saying this; I'm sorry.)

I think if I were a character in that movie
I would be the (unseen) person
texting Stephen Dorff's character:
"you're an asshole."

I don't know what that says about us.

(That's a lie because I do (know).)

Today I Read a Book of Poems by a Young Woman and They Reminded Me of You (Or of Your Poems)

I felt possessive of you in a way
I hadn't
since 2009 or 2010,
maybe
it seemed obvious (to me)
your influence on her

a couple of her poems
contained the phrase 'jump-kick'
which seems like a phrase
that should have been copyrighted by you
or something

the first time I met this young woman
we were in a group
and the group was playing that game
where you list people you would like to have sex with
and at the top of this young woman's list
was you
and I wondered
if you had ever
been in a similar group
playing a similar game
and if anyone had ever
said my name

but I realized pretty quickly
how unlikely it would be
for you to be in such a situation
since you hate groups
and playing games
and talking about people
you would like to have sex with

Seven Years

someone on the radio or in a podcast—I forget which
said something about lee Strasburg telling actors to only use memories that were seven
years old or older to help them conjure emotions for acting a scene.
Strasburg thought memories less than seven years old were too raw still to be used
creatively or artfully and I realized upon hearing that theory that everything I have
written about us has been written well under the seven year mark and perhaps this is why
it cannot be viewed as art, why my friend M. said I should wait,

But how do I calculate?
From the time we met or the time we stopped talking?
It is only a year difference but still it seems important to know

One of my mother's boyfriends—the piano player—said the same thing about heroin. Not
that you can write about it in seven years but that if you can make it through seven years
of an addiction you will lose your addiction.

I wonder if that is accurate and if the same thing can be said about a relationship such as
ours and if so that would mean I only have another two years (if you count the year we
met) or three more (if you count the year we stopped speaking).

And either way: there is an endpoint and I am preemptively sad for that endpoint to arrive.

I Am Sorry Nothing I Have Written about Us Yet Can Be Construed as 'Art'

Last night was the night I volunteer at the barn
I feel like you would think more highly of me if you saw me there
Which is why I choose not to tell you about anything I do that could be construed as
    'good'—like volunteering with children and animals

Actually, that's not true. Anything I said up until now.
I don't think your opinion of me would be changed.
I think your opinion of me is static.
And I don't mean that negatively or positively.

I am going to nominate all of my exes for Pushcarts this year
I don't know if I should consider you 'my ex' but for what it's worth
I am going to nominate you too,
If only because I know how much you will hate it.

I Am Going to Nominate All My Exes for Pushcarts RN

I have emailed several of your friends and so far not one has told
Me anything new about you
I don't think they know you at all
(though they pretend 'for the camera' or for 'posterity,' otherwise)

I remember sucking in my breath.
When I touched your chest in the front seat of my car
There was a field not far beyond the car and I told you to go there
When I left you were sitting on the ground, waiting on the bus,
And I've never seen a person look so defeated.

Or *desolate*.

I need to look up the definition for the word 'desolate' but even without being certain of
the meaning, that's the word I attribute to the way your face looked the last time I saw
you in my home state.

'Desolate' is also the feeling I get when I think of you now as I nominate a story you wrote
for a Pushcart.

I think I have exhausted the point at which my audience wants to hear about you or us or whatever

Last week I was visiting my daughter at her university and I asked how long someone can stay in a room, like, a visitor, like, how many consecutive nights. I told her I wanted to know this because I was writing a story in which a mother stays in her son's dorm room for a long time and this was the reason I gave myself also (for asking) but I think in truth I wanted to know because I have a genuine interest in staying in my daughter's dorm room for an infinite amount of time in response to this existential crisis I am having

I am going to email you now

I told myself that when I finished this collection of poems I could email you
Emailing you was a goal I gave myself like losing weight or cleaning four and a half
    bathrooms in one afternoon

Let's take a bath together

I have never met a single person who has been inside your house
Sometimes I fantasize about hiring a private detective to tell me all of the things I want to
    know about you that no one knows but I don't know what those things are

What do you want to know? you said once. *Ask me anything and I'll tell you.*
It was like you had granted me an exclusive interview.
But I didn't know what I wanted to know so I didn't ask you anything

Maybe instead I want to be the private detective
Not to determine pieces of information about your life
But in order to have a reason for following you

I want to observe you in all your natural settings
Without you knowing you are being observed
And then I want to observe you again
But this time you will know I am there
But both of us will pretend I am not
And in this manner we will not grow tired of one another
Or take each other for granted

Today I hope a bus accidentally kills me

A couple months ago I had a dream you overdosed and all of us were gathered in a vigil
      outside your apartment
I remember being really angry with you that you had done that
Because I was still heavily invested in writing about us and by dying
You had ended my book for me
Which made me feel like you were back in control again

It seems funny we were gathered outside your apartment
Since none of us has ever been to your apartment
And none of us knows where you live

I remember standing outside your apartment
Maybe I was holding a candle
Maybe it was just a cigarette
I remember thinking, *I wonder if his mother will give me our emails*
So I can assemble them in a book
Like letters between dead poets of the past
Only I would still be of the present

I don't know your mother but I think she would let me
If this happens
Maybe you can ask her now ahead of time
Give her my email address
Explain to her I won't be needing the nudes back
I kept copies of those
Unlike the emails you wrote me
I have been unable to look at the ones I wrote you
To know if I deleted them or not
It's an *embarrassment of riches*
I have never used that term before now
I never thought I would use it with you
In regard to us
I'm not even really sure what it means

How will I know now if you are dead
Will you ask your mother to email me that too

I can't keep explaining your story of origin to my father-in-law

What happened to the promise of violence
The *summer of sam*
Or was it *son of sam*

I waited four and a half years for you to make your presence known
In my kitchen
To watch you die of a self inflicted stab wound on my hardwood floor
It had been replaced once already
A leaky refrigerator we were told by the real estate woman who sold us this house
Your only real intimacy with it, the banana you scraped off the grain for me
The night of the party at which we first found ourselves intimate
In a chair I sit in every day, never thinking of our intimacy
Or thinking of it only when writing poems to you or about you (is there a difference?)

That was the first time you lied to me
You said, "don't worry, pretty baby, there will be plenty of time for us"

Do you know that third important Russian novelist

Not Tolstoy or Dostoyevsky but another one
This one was born in 1818
I remember this fact but not the author's name
I was reading an introduction to this author's novella *First Love*
After another author recommended it in the new york times book review last Sunday
That author said it was the best love story of all time
Last night I got drunk from a single beer
I failed to notice the alcohol content, which was 11%
I was listening to tom sizemore on the bret easton ellis
Podcast and I didn't realize I was drunk
I just kept putting my hand over my heart
And attributing the action to how endeared to mr sizemore I was
Anyhow, in the intro to the Russian novelist's novella
It was stated of him, the Russian author, that he fell in love with a married opera singer
    and that the . . . lasted a lifetime
'he was a narcissist in love with his own love'
was something like the sentence that followed
I believe I am unable to tell if I am in love with you or myself in a similar fashion
As the Russian novelist
I have not finished the introduction and do not know if the author ever married another
    woman
I do not know if tom sizemore is married currently or if he ever was
As far as I know you are not married but how would I know if you were

What is an existential crisis if you feel you are having one every day

I don't think I would ever tell my daughter anything again after I told her I was thinking
of taking a part time job and she told me she didn't want me to work
Sometimes my daughter can be like a possessive boyfriend
I said, 'is it because you want me to always be available to visit you'
And she said, 'no, it's not that' but I'm pretty sure she was lying

Sometimes I think about how she would react if I didn't text her back for forty-eight
hours and I become nervous in the way a woman becomes nervous when she has a
possessive boyfriend

I think if you and I were ever together in a real sense you would act like a possessive
boyfriend or maybe I would (act like a possessive gf)

You would know all my tendencies toward deceit and would concoct some even when
there were none

My husband and I get along because he (mostly) does not think too hard about what I am
doing or observe me in the manner in which you and my daughter observe me

I think in some real ways I miss the feeling of being possessed.
I think this is my 'main problem in life' currently

Tanja

Tanja says I am too controlled
Which is ironic because I was just saying I felt a real lack of control
In my life

"Your life is kind of claustrophobic," she said
or maybe I said that to her, about my life, and she agreed.

"I don't think it's good for you to not talk to someone you want to talk to," Tanja said.

She said, "I believe jealousy is 100% the responsibility of the jealous person."

Tanja was saying all the things I wanted to hear and the exact opposite

Of what everyone else was saying.

Naturally my impulse was to listen to Tanja and to ignore the others.

I forget if it was before or after this that I replied to your text in a humorous manner

I think I make exceptions for humor

I think I believe I don't have to feel guilty if everything I say to you can be construed
    as funny

If you told me you would never stop loving me I wouldn't believe you

If you were less attractive maybe I could believe anything you say
what you said was, your feelings for me will never change
I told you the same thing and I think you believed me because
I am not that beautiful
Or I am not so beautiful that it seems impossible I will not stop loving you.
I think your face looks most beautiful in the lighting at the KGB Bar
Though I read there once and did not find the lighting to be all that
Flattering
I have never posted the pictures of myself at the KGB Bar but I sometimes
Watch the video of your reading on mute
I guess I care less what you have to say
Or what you have to say is unbelievable or something.

I think I want to say something about patti smith and mapplethorpe now

I started reading *just kids*, finally, after reading another magazine article on patti
It opens with patti recalling her last conversation with robert before he died
He was in the hospital and she phoned him

I think it is unfair of our current culture to expect me to no longer
Be your friend now that I am married
I'm sorry I agreed to that

I am often so worried about my morality I forget about your wellbeing

The thing I hate about my friend y is she only seems to find it necessary to stay in touch
    with me when I am 'going through something' but I think I need her as
Much or more during the times I am not going through anything
Or at least, that's when I feel loneliest

Every man I have ever lived with has stopped wanting to have sex with me

Today I found porn on my roommate's computer
Actually, it was a shared iPad
I do not look at my roommate's computer
(You understand here that by 'roommate' I mean *husband*)

I was unsure how to process this
If I should be mad or jealous or accusatory
Mostly I was grateful he had fucked up too
So often I feel like I'm the only one
Who is fucking up

I had wanted to have sex last night with my husband (as a way to deal with the guilt I felt
        re talking to you, maybe) and he was too tired
But now I realize he had looked at porn yesterday afternoon
While I was visiting my daughter even though we had previously
Discussed the role porn was playing in our lives and how it seemed like often he would
        rather masturbate to porn than have sex with me or watch porn
While having sex with me
(or was that a conversation a husband and wife had in a movie I watched recently on
        iTunes, I forget; probably it was both)

I guess I failed to notice how porn has become such a large part of our life

I felt less guilty about talking to you yesterday when I saw the porn on the shared iPad

I had felt like crying re the amount of guilt I had felt talking to you

I feel like crying a lot lately

Yesterday during lunch with my daughter I thought I was going to have to leave the table and go into the bathroom like Franny in *Franny & Zooey* but then the moment passed and I was 'okay' again

We went back to my daughter's dorm room and sat on her futon and watched a
    competitive weight loss show and I contemplated texting you

I texted you and then I texted my husband and I wasn't sure if that made me feel better
    or worse

I felt like I was going to throw up a lot yesterday

I ate six bites of my turkey roll up and then moved food around my plate

I don't necessarily want to stay married and be unable to be with you but I don't
    necessarily want to be divorced either

My mother let her hair grow out and now she says it is yellow and she can no longer look
    in the mirror

In twenty years I will be the age my mother is currently

My mother hasn't had sex in fifteen years and she and my stepfather just celebrated their
    twentieth wedding anniversary

I am already unable to look in mirrors

Last time my daughter and I were in sunglass hut I kept trying on sunglasses and asking
    my daughter how they looked

The woman who worked there was persistently trying to get me to hold a mirror and look
    into it

Finally I told her I have a phobia of mirrors - that I don't look into them and she backed
    away behind the counter and I could tell she did not like me anymore

I think mostly I am afraid of being alone which is odd since I like being alone so much

At some point while writing this I finally replied to your email and I'm sorry I failed to mention this sooner

I'm glad I didn't know you had a 'breakdown'
Ten days before I finally emailed you back
I wouldn't have wanted my motivation for emailing you to be (construed as) anything
      other than my own selfish reasons for wanting to talk to you
You were making a lot of jokes when we talked and seemed 'upbeat'
I cried every day for two weeks before my daughter went to college two months ago
I don't know if I had a breakdown but I fully expect to at any moment
Today I texted you about something that was troubling me
I had been manic all morning, texting five different people the same thing
Finally I texted you and immediately when I read your response I felt calm
In a way I hadn't with the five other people's responses
I kept thinking I was going to help you through this tough time you were going through
      but I think it is you who are helping me and maybe in that way I *am* helping you
      after all. I don't know.

Eugene O'Neill

I think you could be a great playwright
I never thought my husband could be great at anything
Except teaching and being a stepfather and loving me,
All worthy causes.

I would have to treat you differently, is what I mean, like a great artist
Whereas currently I am the 'great artist' in the house (even though I am not that great)
I don't know if two great artists can live under one roof

(last year you told me they could but you said a lot of things last year that never amounted
        to anything except these poems)

My husband doesn't like to discuss things much
He likes drinking beer with the guys late at night
With me he will rarely stay up past eleven

Eugene O'Neill was a great artist but a shitty husband

Eugene O'Neill said something like, you can only blame yourself so much before turning
        the blame on someone else

I guess in that regard I am a great artist also
(and also a shitty husband)

Too soon

I think it is too soon to talk about how our talking will make us feel
I have been listening to music a lot more the last four days again
(Instead of podcasts or instead of watching tv)
And it feels good to relate to music in this way again
I have increased my cigarette intake from two cigarettes a night to three
These are the only differences my husband could possibly notice if he were at all
  perceptive or curious about me.
I spend a significant amount of time alone.

First thought, best thought, or whatever that was jack Kerouac said

I think if I were ever going to publish these poems
I would have to edit them first
But editing these poems does not interest me
As a reader I like to read poems that feel unedited
But when you say a collection of poems feels unedited
Someone always assures you that you are wrong
That that is how good the poet is
That they make you feel the poems are raw and unworked
But in reality they have probably been worked a lot

Maybe I am uninterested in working currently
I have always had tendencies for laziness
And apathy
If I weren't so lazy I would probably be with you now
But disrupting my life (again) is something that no longer interests me
Or interests me less than sitting quietly in my chair and reading a book

I think it would be fair to say you felt similarly five years ago
After I disrupted my life for you (or in accordance with you or something) and you did not
    react similarly

I would often text you to ask what you were doing on a particular night and you would
    say you were working or sitting on the couch reading
And I related both of those acts to how you were not coming to see

I am good at relating everything in some manner back to me.

Elliott Smith Songs

I showed what I had of these poems to a young poet friend of mine
And he said they reminded him of Elliott Smith songs
I have never listened to Elliott Smith but I have an appreciation
For his death like most people

Maybe our talking will be good for my marriage

I hate feeling representative of a cliché
That is the worst part of talking to you again

The first time I typed this title I typed, "maybe our talking will be good for *our* marriage"

Oops!

My husband and I had good sex two nights ago and I wasn't sure if I should attribute this
to talking to you

I had felt happier, less anxious, that day as a result of our text messages in the afternoon

I don't know if it would be true to say I think of you less now that we are talking

But I think it would be true to say I think of you with less urgency now that we are talking

The difference between me six years ago and me now

the person who remains not bored in a marriage is the person least secure in the marriage
and with this in mind I know the least bored person in our marriage would be me
which is why I would never marry you

I do not think my husband is ever bored of me

Overboard is a movie my mother and her boyfriend watched a lot when we lived in a shitty two bedroom apartment in Arizona

I realized when thinking about the *Overboard* type scenario we talked about in text messages yesterday that in movies they never show extended family members because the extended family members would unnecessarily complicate the plot but in reality—if you did impregnate one woman three times or three women one time and were able somehow, through the women's untimely deaths or bad characters—extreme drug usage or whatever, to take custody of the children and I were to help you raise them, we would still have the women's parents to contend with and maybe the women's sisters and brothers also who would probably want to take active roles as grandparents and aunts and uncles and that would be annoying or bothersome or something

We were discussing the *Overboard* scenario as well as the *Raising Arizona* one (in which we kidnap rich people's babies and raise them as our own) because (though neither of us said this outright) I am probably too old to have your child now even if we were in a place to have a child, which we are not.

You said you were standing in line at a Dunkin' Donuts and a two year old with pig tails was in front of you, looking backward at you, and the way you described this two year old I had to tell you to stop in the same way I used to, five years ago, tell you to stop when you were saying things to make me sexually aroused, only this time you were arousing my heart in a way that was more painful than the sexual arousal had been.

Also, there is no way of alleviating the sort of pain that arouses your heart; not that I know of anyway

I said, "I was put on this earth to mother"

I said, "I will mother you if you let me"

If we had had sex six years ago we could have made a baby

I read a statistic that half of all marriages end after a child dies or is kidnapped but maybe the statistic only applied to deaths not kidnappings

It is probably harder to get statistics on kidnappings

I think the Lindberghs stayed together

Though I don't really know

I don't even know if they found the Lindbergh baby dead or alive

I'm going to Google that now

Instead of thinking about how my eggs are too old now to produce the baby I assumed we would have six years ago

Something I Failed to Mention

I am now—in October of 2014—a hated member of our community
I think that's important to finally address
Friends have turned their backs on me
My husband is kind but unpracticed at acts of outrage or empathy or courage
He pats my knee, offers a pitying look.
Today I waited until he left the room to text you
Normally I feel disloyal talking to you when he is in the house
Today I felt justified ignoring all sense of moral decency

I want to reincarnate as a small female cat so that you can give
Me a southern woman's name; this is what I tell you in the text I send
When my husband leaves the room.

You have two female cats with southern names already.
I will be the first and last person I know to see where you sleep.
It would be not unlike being taken home by Edgar Allen Poe.

Let the Right One In

I received an email from M. after M. read these poems

M. said, "I wouldn't publish these"

M. said, "In some of the poems you address him directly"

M. said, "You write about texting him while L. is in the house"

M. said all of these things as though I was not the author of the poems, as though I was unfamiliar with them or had forgotten what I had written

She said, "I think hurting someone with your writing is only warranted when the writing is very, very good."

It was clear M. didn't think my poems were very good; it was clear she didn't think I would be winning any prizes!

Later I received an email from J.

J. said, "I think you should cut down the number of poems about —— "

J. said, "You have a novel about —— and over a hundred poems about —— "

I knew I should feel embarrassed about having written so many pages about ——

I wanted to tell J. that was the point; how boring obsession can be, even to the obsessed, but how unrelenting also, even in the face of boredom

It felt odd to me sometimes when I thought of my husband having no one to obsess over

How much pressure that put on me!

I *am* a strong woman; that's what my female friends don't get!

Everything I have ever written for the last fifteen years has been about running away but I'm still here

My daughter makes all my runaway fantasies impossible

Anyway, I can't imagine us ever spending more than forty-eight hours together because we never have

I could take a tiny shit-hole of an apartment in your city and still you would refuse to see me

Which is why I stay here and text you from my husband's and my bedroom.

I sleep in a sleeping bag on the floor to remind me of (what?)

I don't know (you?)

Donald Hall Has Nothing to Complain About

One of my 'supporters,' a male poet in his sixties,

Sent me an article he wrote about his 'old friend' Donald Hall yesterday

"I sent our correspondences to *The Paris Review* recently," he told me

I had never thought one way or the other about Donald Hall

I only barely knew his name

I was ignorant of poetry and poets other than Bukowski and they are trying to erase ole
     Bukowski now too

I read the opening paragraph of the article

There was mention of a book of poems

I got my Kindle to look for it

I couldn't find the one mentioned but I found another one and downloaded a sample

I read the first three poems—that was all you got with the free sample—

So I bought the book

I read the same three poems again and then I read two more

Donald Hall wanted me to feel sorry for him; his wife was dying of Leukemia,
a noble disease

Everyone loved and mourned her dying with him

I didn't see what there was to feel sorry about

I had a hard time leaving my bed and after that I had a hard time leaving my room

My hair hadn't fallen out but I had lost five pounds

I had been obsessed with the same asshole for five years

No one liked the asshole I was obsessed with

I wasn't a very sympathetic figure either

Taken out of context—which was the only way people seemed to be taking me—I was an asshole, also

I wanted to read old Donald Hall tell me about a time his wife had fallen out of love with him or cheated on him or a time he had cheated on her or not wanted to have sex with her or resented her

Instead, all Donald Hall wanted to do was tell me how perfect his wife was, how angelic

I got a drink and went down into the basement to drink it

I didn't want to think about Donald Hall's wife anymore

I hoped I was never dying of cancer/ I didn't want to be so simplistically portrayed

Fine Young Cannibals

When M. wrote me about these poems she wrote me about how I didn't have it as bad as I was making it out; that I wasn't as hated as I was portraying myself on the page

She was saying in so many words, "Get over yourself!"

It was a little hard to take from a person who'd told me she'd posted a link to my essay the day it went up and two hours later had taken it back down

"I couldn't take all that outrage directed at me," M. had said.

"It had surprised me," she'd said

I didn't think M. was qualified to tell me how bad I did or didn't have it

M. was, as usual, living with an older man

M. was well taken care of

The sister of a famous actor was optioning her novel to be made into a movie

I'm not trying to sound like Marc Maron here but yeah I'm bitter sometimes!

My husband is so nice and even-keeled

I am entertaining *Natural Born Killers* type fantasies again:
Mickey and Mallory

I remember that movie came out right after I married my first husband

Shortly after, we sold all our furniture and bought a van for five hundred dollars
And camped our way westward across the country

It felt similar to what we had seen in *Natural Born Killers* without the roadside killings

Same crappy motel interiors
Same desert landscape, same campfire hallucinations

When I texted you four nights ago in the midst of another despair
I asked if I should leave the literary world and when I woke in the morning
I saw your reply:
   'fuck yes please!'

You had already done so a few weeks earlier
Before the scandal unfolded;
   the rumor of a 'breakdown'

You seem happy to be a person I am consulting
To be a person capable of helping me
I don't think you would like it the other way around

My husband seems too impassionate to leave the lit world with me

My husband is very even-keeled

It Is Unfair to compare my relationship with my husband to my relationship with you because one of you is not real

I didn't want my husband to take a stand publicly on my behalf

We had discussed this; we had come to a mutual agreement

Most of the time I was ' fine' with our agreement

One night I was inconsolable, sobbing on our bedroom floor

"Why can't you be irrational?" I yelled. "Why are you always so calm and steady?"

I wanted my husband to be overcome with anger.

I wanted his anger to overcome his rational side.

My husband just sat on the bed staring at me
My husband didn't have an answer
My husband said, "I don't know. I'm sorry."

It was an unfair comparison but I compared him to you.

I thought you would stand up for me publicly,
Even if I asked you not to,
If we were ever together IRL, I mean

In my fantasy version of us this seemed like a plus

Even though in reality I don't think it would be.
In reality you and I would always be fighting.

I envisioned us fighting at parties and outside your
Workplace; I envisioned us fighting so much
That the neighbors called the cops

Maybe that is something I remember from *Barfly*
Mickey Rourke and Faye Dunaway were always fighting
The cops were always being called

The scene I remember most vividly though is the one
Where they eat an ear of corn right off the stalk

Faye Dunaway vomits or spits the corn onto the ground

I am forever torn before a fantasy version of my life—
Based on other writers' lives I have witnessed in movies—
And my own.

Maybe it is something I remember from my childhood:

The time my mother and her boyfriend were arrested for fighting outside the bar they
both worked at in Mesa, Arizona; my mother and her boyfriend resisting arrest, running
from the cops

I wonder how they will portray me a hundred years from now -
if you will even be in the movie.

Currently I cannot tell if my tooth hurts or if I am only imagining it
I cannot decide if I should drink alcohol tonight or only tea

My husband is at a university in Kentucky
And you are working at a bar I don't know the name of
It is possible my ear hurts also
My hypochondria inflates when my husband is not in the house
You are a hypochondriac also
Each of the last two times I saw you, you complained of fever
And earache

In this way we would be competing, also

We would never stop being in competition for which one of us hurts more

Blonde Ambition

M. said no one thinks of how they will be portrayed when they are dead

What she meant was I was an extreme narcissistic for thinking it

I didn't think I was an extreme narcissist, though

I thought most writers thought this way

If they had any belief in themselves at all

If they had any ambition or an ego or whatever

A *Simple Plan* Is a Movie starring Billy Bob Thorton, Not Something I know Anything About

The first night we texted after four and a half years of not texting I told myself would be
the last.

My husband was out of town then too.

My husband is always reading at universities and festivals and on panels.

I have never been on a panel in my life

I don't think you have either

One time during the time we were not talking I saw that you were going to one of the
Scandinavian countries (Finland?) and I was proud of you for flying that far.

I wanted to go with you, of course.

I wanted to email you and tell you how proud of you I was.

The best I could do was email the man who publishes all your books and hope it got back
to you (my pride).

It was mid August of this year when you emailed me and mid September the night I
texted you.

You called me 'girl' just like men do in country songs.

I remember leaving the room to cry in my bathroom.

My bathroom seemed a more appropriate room in which to cry.

I left my phone in the kitchen where I had been sitting while texting you.

You said everything perfect that night as though your dialogue had been scripted (by me).

You told me everything I wanted to hear and I fell asleep happy.

I smiled into my pillow as I had the time a year earlier when you'd mentioned my cat on
your blog.

I was satisfied with our (single night) interaction.

I promised myself I would not text you again

I told myself I now had the closure I'd sought for four years

Then the next day there was a new text from you

It said "are you coming to —— on your tour?"

I had entered your name in my phone as a female

Acquaintance of mine and at first I thought it was the female

Acquaintance texting me to ask if I was going to ——

And that didn't make sense.

I thought, 'why is —— asking me if we are coming to —— when —— lived in new
york city?"

Then I remembered it wasn't actually —— who was texting me but you and I smiled and
ignored my plan to only text with you once and replied 'yes'

Of course this was the last time you texted me without me texting you first,
That I can remember

Tour Poems

A.

I can no longer remember the specifics of our communications
At the beginning of tour.
That was a month ago now
I wish I were the type to keep a journal.
I remember we were in L.A. first
I remember texting you one night at 11 and you not responding until
2 pm the next afternoon
I remember wondering if you had been with a woman
I think I felt like crying; it's possible even I cried.

I was staying at a famous Hollywood hotel
I thought you would hate it but I told you anyway
'I bet you bought a new suit for the pool,' you said
you called me 'candyass' which felt like anyone else calling me 'honey'

I can't imagine publishing this while still married
Maybe this is my effort at not being in control
I don't want to make any more decisions
Or be responsible for anyone else's happiness
That's why I got divorced the first time
(I was uncomfortable being the one making the decision to drive to the hospital . . . or to
        dole out medication.)

I remember the reading in L.A. being very emotional (for me)
It was the first time I had appeared in public since the 'scandal'
I read from my novel
I read a sad part about you and Mexico and not talking to you anymore after Mexico
I got emotional reading it
My voice shook but not like it did when I first started reading in public
It felt like a strong performance
Some people complimented me and I wished I had the nerve to read in front of you . . .

I didn't read from my novel at any other stop on tour, though

I didn't understand how actors gave the same live performance every night on Broadway
I was exhausted from just one

Later, when we were playing ping pong back at the Chateau
I tried imagining you staying there with me

I try to imagine you and I traveling everywhere together
I don't understand why you can't see how awesome we would be
We wouldn't have to kill anyone or do any drugs.
That's not what I mean.
Or is it? I can't tell anymore.

B.

Once I got back to the Midwest you asked me when we would be stopping in your city
I hadn't thought about it in a while.
It felt still far off.
I started to say two weeks from Friday and then I realized it was only
Five days away.
I felt panicky and anxious.
I didn't know what I would wear.
"you can't come to the reading," I said and you said 'why not'
"you told me once, five years ago, not to come to yours. It seems only fair." I said.
You said you didn't remember saying this.
You said "that doesn't sound right"
"A woman doesn't forget something like that," I said. "But anyway it doesn't matter
    anymore."
I knew even five years ago I could have gone to your reading if I had wanted to. If I
    had wanted to, nothing you could have said would have stopped me. I hoped you
    respected me more than that. I didn't think I could read in front of you without
    vomiting. If I saw you I would run away.

We had to bypass your city on our way to our first stop.
I texted you that we were passing through.
It was two days before the reading in your city.
You seemed excited, manic.
You used more exclamation points than I could remember you using.
You called me 'baby' or 'babe', I forget which.
You said you would take us to a concert.
You said you were getting off work at eight.

Everything sounded perfect and I spent the next forty-eight hours discussing the morality
    and ethics of the situation with my tour mates; what I was willing to do and what
    I wasn't.

The night of the reading in your city we had agreed to go to dinner with a friend who
    hadn't met you.
She had read my novel (about you) but I didn't tell her about meeting up with you later. I
    didn't want her to know on account of the potential for her judging me.

I was more serious and quieter at dinner because of the sporadic way in which you were
     texting me.
The mania of two days before was gone; no more exclamation points.
I was surprised you were texting me at all.
I was beginning to feel something I would categorize as despondency.
It seemed inevitable you wouldn't show.

After a dinner that seemed prolonged and never ending we dropped my friend at her
     apartment and drove back downtown to our hotel, which was the same hotel you had
     met me at twice before

I was touring with three other women one of whom had mentioned wanting to see you,
     months earlier, when we had discussed what cities we would go to.
('The only city I care about is ―――― because I want to see ―――― .')
At the time I had been uncomfortable with you being contacted.
You and I still had not talked in four years.
I had said no to readings I knew you were part of, avoided you in other ways also.
Our original tour lineup did not include your city.
It was added later. before you and I started talking again.
I can't remember why.

By the time we returned to the hotel I felt unhopeful you would show.
WE took bets in the elevator.
You were still saying you would come.
You said you hadn't gotten off work yet even though it was after eight o'clock.
"What would his motivation be for not coming?" C. said.
She doesn't know you as well as I do.

We sat in a booth in the lobby of the hotel.
I was remembering the argument you'd had with another friend of mine in the same
     hotel lobby.
I ordered a cocktail and tried not to look at my phone.
You stopped responding to my texts at some point.
I remember thinking I should have been more surprised or embarrassed or disappointed
I remember saying, "well, now I don't have to worry about my morality or ethics")

I still hadn't heard from you by early afternoon of the following day.
I knew you were probably feeling shitty about what had happened or not happened or
     about yourself.
I waited until we were no longer in your city to text you.
We had stopped at a Cracker Barrel and I was sitting in a rocking chair on the front porch.
I said something like, "it's okay, I'm not mad at you."
(I don't remember what else I said.)

(that's not true. I remember saying 'I still love you' also)
I had found a chocolate advent calendar for my daughter.
The other women were still inside the Cracker Barrel shopping.

I don't feel like disclosing what you said in reply.
It is shocking even to myself (that I don't want to disclose everything in my life in my
　　writing; that I reserve anything for myself (or for you) at all).

We piled back in the van.
Someone put in The National and then they put in Coldplay

We were on our way to Indiana, the home state of James Dean

　　c.
In Indianapolis a woman refused to host our reading because of something I'd written
　　about my (half) sister, a disclosure I'd made, something from my childhood.
The gallery manager said we could still read there though
So we did but it was an odd atmosphere.
I could feel the presence of the woman, 'Wendy;'
mid-reading a black woman entered, her entire face painted.
I wondered if it was a protest of some kind
I never saw her speak—maybe it was a silent protest
I was wearing a crop top with the word 'selfie' across the chest.
I thought my daughter would be horrified.
You had been texting me more than ever since I left your state.
You were back to texting me manically, the way you had two days before I was to read in
　　your city.
I could tell you felt safer again now, with me out of the way.
You felt comfortable again calling me 'baby'
It amazed me how patient and accepting of you I was now
That I was married
Or now that I understood you better or understood 'us' better.
Who else but us would feel 'good' about *not* seeing each other
The night before?
I was done fighting (you).
I was in love with the illusion of you, the illusion of us.
But isn't that how all relationships work?
My relationship with my husband, for instance?
My husband knowingly sets aside information he has gathered
About me in order to continue to love me.
It is the same way for me with you.

D.

Midway through our tour we stopped back in my hometown for a night
We were reading at a local bookstore
Another woman had dropped out of that reading also
I was growing more unpopular the longer I talked to you . . .

C. put in the Dan Savage podcast.
It was midnight already.
I had been driving all day and night.
(I was still the one 'in control' then)

I have never listened to this podcast
C. said she listened every week
I couldn't understand why
Each call was more depressing than the last
A man whose wife had no interest in sex,
A woman whose boyfriend didn't want her to initiate sex or even affection
People in sexless marriages
(it occurred to me while typing this particular poem, that maybe this is a cry for help; that
      neither my husband nor you will be the one in the end to make me happy, that I will
      be forced out on my own, that maybe a third party or third and fourth parties (I am
      not that old, after all) will come into my life . . .)
people in marriages in which the other partner would have sex with them out of duty but
      with no genuine interest on his/her part . . .

Dan Savage's answers were almost always the same
the marriages or relationships were almost always 'doomed'
(I still couldn't understand any of the other people in the van's attraction to this podcast,
      unless it made them feel better about their own sex lives/relationships, which were
      obviously, comparatively 'newer', younger, not anywhere as 'doomed')
unless extreme steps were taken, therapists consulted, major 'work' done,
and who needed that?

I began to feel more and more depressed the longer we drove,
The longer the podcast played.
I was forced to address problems in my marriage I hadn't wanted to think about.

I could have cried.

Instead I got carsick. (something I thought was impossible to get while driving.)

I felt unnaturally nauseous.

I blamed it on the van; an odd, metallic odor in the car.
"DO you guys smell that?"
something burning; wires, maybe. Something related to the heater.

I turned the heater off.
Drove with the window cracked despite the autumn chill.
The remaining hour back to Ann Arbor.

"That was a rough last half hour," C. said when we got home.
I got out the whiskey and my cigarettes and the four of us sat at the dining room table,
    laughing incoherently.

The next day I felt like crying,
like I might at any moment burst into inconsolable tears.
I hid from my husband and tour mates,
spent the majority of the day in my bedroom and bathroom texting you
"just live your life," you said.
"I was trying to live my life in —— ," I said, referring to the night you failed, again, for a
    third time, to meet me in a hotel lobby. (to be fair, the two times before I had sprung
    my presence on you, arrived in your city without warning, like a stalker or a crazy
    person. What worked on my then-boyfriend now husband, didn't work on you.)

(I spend the majority of my time hiding from my husband now; locked up here 'working',
    which feels to me like spending time with you; my work ethic is improving.)

you said, "okay but it's hard to know how to act when you keep changing your mind
    about what you want."

"tell me about it," I said.

    E.
C. said stopping home mid tour was awkward.
"You'll feel better when tour's over and you come home for good," she said.
"One time [her boyfriend who is a musician and in a band] stopped home mid tour to play
    a show and it was awkward. Neither of us knew how to act."

"yeah," I said. I didn't know how to tell C. it was more than that; I was unhappy, and the
    unhappiness was unrecognizable to me until I left home and returned. Maybe it was
    an adjustment to an empty house, now that my daughter was away at college, or
    maybe it was more than that. I didn't know, I just felt crappy. I felt like I didn't want
    to be left alone with my husband, I didn't want to come back without my tour mates.
    I was fantasizing about living in a house with them. Was this a normal way for a
    happily married woman to think? What would Dan Savage have to say about it?

We went to the reading and after the reading we went to a bar and after the bar we went
     to a karaoke place, got a private room.
I sat on one side of the room with my tour mates, singing songs with them,
and my husband sat on the other with various men and sang songs solo or with them.

Later that night, after we got back from karaoke, C. interviewed my husband for our tour
     documentary.
I wasn't in the room at the time but later, on our last day of tour, she showed me the
     footage.
He was drunk, flush-faced. I smiled.
She was asking him how much he would miss me and he said 'a medium amount' but it
     seemed like he was downplaying.
She asked how much he thought I would miss him or home and he said, 'less.'

The footage was hard to watch and endearing . . .
I felt guilty for not missing my husband as much as he missed me

('but you're on tour,' C. said. 'And he's the one waiting at home.' But I had been the one
     at home months earlier, in the middle of summer, and I hadn't missed him all that
     much then either; I had spent my days with my daughter or writing and my evenings
     watching old films, drinking wine, smoking. I had enjoyed my solitude (with the
     luxury of knowing I had a husband who would be returning in a week); I was well
     practiced in the art of being alone.)

I saw for a brief moment the man I fell in love with.

I wanted to miss my husband.

Last night I Thought of a Beautiful Poem in my Head as I Fell Asleep But I Was Too Lazy to Get Up and Write It Down and Now It Is Gone Forever

If my husband were to have an affair with a student or colleague or another writer, our
    sex would benefit in a similar fashion.
I would cling to him more tightly, find him in his university office,
Lock the door. I would fuck him like a student rather than like a wife.
It would be the same if he threatened to leave me again;
Say, because of this book.
We would have the best sex then.

I Am Going to Masturbate Now

I was alone in the house
My husband was in Atlanta, on a panel on women in publishing
He was always asked to be on panels and to read at universities
I couldn't remember the last time I had masturbated (alone) to porn.
(I was never asked to be on panels)
I found a DVD in the back drawer of my closet
There were ten or fifteen costumes in that drawer also and I hadn't worn any in years
I had the impression you wouldn't like me in any sort of costume
You seemed old-fashioned with regard to sex or with regard to sex with me or something
There was a cheerleader and a cowgirl and a stewardess
I liked the stewardess costume best; it was aqua and satiny and shiny
It had a little pillbox hat and gloves to go with it
I pushed aside the costumes looking for the DVD
There was a small glass dildo also
I took both upstairs with me to my office

[unfinished]

When My Husband Got Home the Sex Was Clinical and Perfunctory

I asked him to shower, laid out a towel for him on the counter
I changed into a negligee I had bought for our anniversary trip three months earlier and
     failed to wear, finding it the last night of our vacation still wrapped in tissue paper at
     the bottom of my suitcase
It was not as beautiful as I remembered
My breasts were not as beautiful in it as I remembered
I had the conscious thought that I would be embarrassed to wear the negligee
In front of you
I felt like a paid escort

Once my husband, before we were married, before I met you,
Had gone to a house of prostitution in Nevada

A man he was with was interviewing the madam for a possible book
He wanted to ghostwrite with her

I had told my husband to get some sort of service, not full penetration or intercourse,
But something lesser, a blowjob or handjob or something like that.

He told me later he got a handjob but I realize as I am typing this he could have gotten
     anything; I wouldn't know
I had him describe for me the procedural
I remember it sounding not unlike last night
The woman had him clean himself and dry off.
I performed the act with porn in my laptop
The sex was not unsatisfactory for me
I was able to climax without him inside of me
Though I was unable to get him to climax and in that way
I felt a bit of a failure
I was aware I was exuding a coldness
I did not kiss my husband on the mouth
After we lay there side by side on our backs a long time
He seemed worried
"Are you thinking or just resting?" he said
'I'm just tired, 'I said, which was partially true.

I need a strong-willed man to overpower me

I think we would both be monsters in a real life relationship together
Though when I have brought this up to you, you have said,
"Sweetheart, I don't know what you mean."

Which is exactly the sort of thing a monster would say.

Burroughs

Today I was reading *Naked Lunch* while waiting for you to reply to my text
(I did not really expect you to reply but still I was hopeful)
I sat in my chair in the kitchen for four hours reading about blowjobs and semen and
anal sex.
I read a scene in which a woman attaches a strap on to fuck a man and I imagined myself
fucking my husband similarly
I thought that I would like it and he would like it and because he would like it I would lose
respect for him after or believe him to be a homosexual
Somewhere in the text Burroughs describes pleasure as the release of tension and I
applied that to my own situation and realized that was how I felt on the occasions
you replied to my texts.
I imagined myself exhaling as your name appeared on my phone
I didn't understand how I could have had control for four years and so easily have lost
that control again within a month

Sweet Bird of Youth

The night I watched porn I also watched *sweet bird of youth*
Or rather, I had watched the first half of *sweet bird of youth* the night before
And now I was watching the conclusion

I can't remember now which night I watched porn –
The night of the first half of the movie or the night of the second.

I was depressed by the depiction of an aging actress on screen.

I identified too strongly with all the aging actresses depicted in movies based on
    Tennessee Williams' plays.

Which means, I guess, I identified with Tennessee Williams, and his fears of falling in love
    with younger men.

When I watched porn I didn't identify with anyone.

A Student in Montreal Wrote an Article in which she stated she could not relate to my poems because they were middle class and American

I think this is a knee-jerk Canadian response to anything American
I cannot see how my poems represent the middle class
My poems are about a woman who doesn't work and drives to see her daughter
And hang out with her at her university
My poems are about a woman with so much free time on her hands to read and write
    poems, to watch old movies and read autobiographies
And languish over a man she has not seen in six years and likely will not see again

I hate myself and want to die; j/k!

Today is a day I would smoke 20 cigs if I had less self-control (and part of me wishes I had)

Sometimes I hate myself most for the lack of a lack of control I seem to (not) possess

Like, at that bookstore we met in, finally, where you brought the much younger woman/
girlfriend

Tanja said, "I would have stood in front of him like, 'hi,' forced him to deal with me."

But that sort of behavior would have required a lack of something I didn't know how to
lack, a Courtney Love type lack of . . . , I don't possess

And I guess in this way, too, I am a fraud

But I don't think it matters, anyway

Anyway, you and your new girlfriend look cute together!

U broke my heart with your text about r&b last night

They only give poetry awards to books about death or dying

If you were dead this would be a much better collection
Deep and emotional instead of superficial and boring
I would seem deeper, I mean
As a result of being allowed to grieve (your death)
It is hard to make ppl understand I am grieving your being alive
Currently
Or it seems selfish because I am married or something

I want to blame you for everything
Including the fact that I will never win an award!

If you were to die (Posthumously) after I publish this
Maybe it would carry more weight

It could still be possible for me to win an award—
Is what I am trying to say to you
(hint, hint)

more than an award though would be my ability to get on with this grieving process

right now I feel I am stuck in one of the stages

I might be stuck in the stage in which you fluctuate between wanting to be suffocated by a
     person because you feel so much (for him) and wanting to rip the cranial covering off
     a person (because you feel so much (for him))

My husband and I had sex last night and I can still smell our sex this morning as I write you this poem

Maybe I am saying this because I am still hurt/angry re your text abt r&b

I don't care how many women you sleep with/have sex with

But your text abt r&b was uncalled for and mean

I am too old to get away with this sort of poetry

I am reading a joan didion novel and that is the only thing that helps me forget about you
or deal with the pain resulting from thinking about you

There are so many similarities between joan's novel and mine

All of the random freeway driving, for instance

Also the sleeping outside by the pool

I wish it were summer rn and that I were alone in this house for a month

I wish I were working on my novel instead of writing you these
Goddamn poems

(even though my novel is also about you)

I hate how much I have made my life about you

(that is only a half true statement: I love it also)

I am as ego driven as you are

Maybe I am nothing more than a bored housewife who is also a writer

Was this anne sexton's problem? sylvia plath's?

Some part of me really wishes I could inhale oven gas just to get back at you

Suicide as revenge!

Suicide as proof of feeling!

Suicide as one-upping you in your personal narration/persona/origin story

I know if I text you tonight I will be sorry

I feel like every interesting relationship I engage in now is like the relationship in the movie *Her*.

Is narcissism where you find everyone but yourself boring?

I am bored by everyone but you and me and victor freeze currently

Everything I typed into my phone's note section last night after we texted

"I'm sorry abt last night," I said. "Too much Grand Marnier."

"Grand Marnier," you said. "You chump. Let's be friends!"

I texted you three more times after that and you never responded.

Maybe you were at work.

I was reading Joan Didion.
I was finishing *Play It as It Lays*.
Joan was having the abortion. Or her character was.
I never understand why women seem so affected by them.
I've had two and I never think about either.
Maybe I am a sociopath. Like that woman in *Tampa*.
Maybe you are (but I'm jumping ahead now).

I typed "too much pride between you and I"
Into the notes section of my phone
I knew all the words to the Eminem song by heart;
I couldn't stop thinking of our pride as a motivating factor for all our (shared) anguish

I kept getting up to type more notes. My phone was in my bathroom.
I typed:

Bored but also anxious
The last time I was brilliant
I never said when or why I was 'leaving'
I just wasn't there anymore (for four and a half years)
I should like to be that brilliant again
I will not take the bait. I will remain calm and sober.

I remember all the stories he told me of his exes
(am I a story he tells now?)

.

Abstinence is more boring than languishing in melancholia
But my pride demands it

It was horrible to think of things by these terms
Cynical

That was the last note I typed

I realized this morning, reading my notes, how boring other ppl's love affairs really are

maybe I will get lucky and a horse will stomp me

I told you I wanted you to suffocate me . . .
This was last Monday (today is Sunday)
Things were going so well then (early last week)

You had just returned from L.A. two days before

You said, "Don't make me crush you. I boxed K's son when I was in L.A. I still got it."

I was very specific in my instructions. I said, "I want you to meet me in a hotel and hug
me for an extended period of time, slowly and gradually increasing pressure until you
ultimately suffocate me. then you can do with my body what you want, *Child of God*
style, take me back to your apartment, pick out lingerie for me, dress me up, before I
disintegrate, before I begin to smell . . . "

Okay, I didn't type all of that.

The first thirty-seven words or so only.

The rest was implied (I think)

I was on my way to volunteer at a therapeutic riding center

I said, "maybe I'll get lucky and a horse will stomp me"

I think this was the manner in which I was dealing with my unaddressed sexual
repression: with fantasies of suffocation and crushing (at the hands of you or the hooves
of a horse or whatever)

You told me once you have a fear of horses
I thought that was so 'cute'
A tough urban guy like you . . .

When you got back from L.A. we were texting.
You said, "[the California] women like them some real Midwest men."

I said, 'oh! are we having a baby!?'
I said, 'I could use 'a real man.' where is one"
And you said, "right here, butthead"

And I said, "a fat lot of good that does me."

And you said, "a fat lot of good!"

And I smiled.

Like I said, things were going so well early last week . . .

Horrible Person

I was watching an episode of *The Kardashians* in my basement
It was one in the morning and I was drinking red wine
It was the episode in which Kim and Kanye get married

Kim's 'best friends' were having a dinner for her in Paris a couple nights before the wedding
Everyone was going around the table and telling stories about Kim
(Most of the stories were about Kanye too)

I noticed the word 'obsessed' was used a lot

"Kanye was *obsessed* with Kim for years"
"Kanye was *obsessed* with Kim from the first moment he met her"
"Kim and Kanye are equally *obsessed* with each other"
"I just think it's so great that two people so *obsessed* with each other are finally getting
     married . . . "

(these aren't direct quotes. I can't remember exactly what was said last night. I was
     drinking a lot of red wine to deal with the fact that I wasn't allowing myself to text
     you (again).)

Naturally I thought about you and me, how if we had any friends, they would probably
     say we've been *obsessed* with each other since 2009.

(I don't know what else to say.
It's just an observation.
I might be hungover.
I'm still not going to text you.)

Kanye wrote Kim a song with the word 'awesome' in it like a hundred times. They played
     it during the episode I watched last night.

(I am still waiting for you to dedicate a book to me.)

I know you think I'm awesome but it would be nice for everyone else to know

I am a horrible person for writing these poems.

I am going to end up alone as punishment for writing these poems.

I am going to end up alone as punishment for being *obsessed* with a horrible person.

I am a horrible person for hurting people I care about because I am too *obsessed* with you to care enough about them to not hurt them.

Maybe you could write me a poem with the words 'horrible person' in it like a hundred times.

'He Is Helen'

The night before I had texted you and you hadn't texted me
I was watching *The Song Remains the Same*
I wasn't drinking (alcohol is not the problem) but the movie was highly sexual. Robert
    Plant's moaning . . .
Jimmy Page . . .

the night before J had said, "I like these poems. In some ways you are subverting the
    patriarchy"

I said "English, please. Speak English"

.

J had an M.FA.

J went to school in New York City

J said, "You are making him an idea of a person. An ideal."

J said, "He is Helen."

J said, "he is an object, you are objectifying him."

I said, "I am?"

I didn't even know. I wasn't sure I agreed. I didn't think writing obsessively about an
    obsession made the object of an obsession 'an object.'

I liked the idea of you as an object, though

I liked the idea of you as an object, but I didn't think I agreed.

11/27/2014

(Alcohol Is Not the Problem)

Black Friday

Today is the day I removed your contact info from my phone
I wrote your number on a piece of paper and stuck that piece of paper in a drawer in the
    back of my closet 'just in case'
I felt like sobbing removing your contact info from my phone but I couldn't sob because
    my family was in my house
I couldn't cut myself because my family was in my house
I could sulk or drink or turn off my phone or go for a two hour drive because my family
    was in my house

This is the only way things were different from five years ago.

The Day Richard Burton Died He Mailed a Letter to Elizabeth Taylor

I said, "we both want what we can't have"
And you said, "how about that"

DATE RAPE

I was on my bed; we were texting
I took a picture of my cat and sent it to you
You sent me a picture of your cat, too.

You were explaining something for me I didn't think needed explaining
You were saying, "they gave me all these drugs until I was basically blacked out."
It felt like you were justifying something to me; I'd heard that rumor also.
I didn't care what you did with Phoebe or Miranda.
I didn't know how to shrug my shoulders in a text so I said, "makes no difference to me."
I was more curious now that you had brought it up, though.
I made a note to ask Miranda about that night; about Phoebe.

I wanted to ask Phoebe directly but I knew I never would.
I wasn't sure if it would make things easier or harder if she told me things you told her
    and they were the same things you told me.

I knew as soon as I saw "sex doesn't matter much to me anymore" in Phoebe's Liveblog
    that she had been hanging around you.

"I wish you wouldn't talk about power. I feel powerless around you," you told me once.
    I wasn't sure if power and control were the same things or different. I felt a lack of
    control with regard to you. I couldn't figure out if that was the same thing.

Ray

On the back of a hotel notepad is a phone number for a man named 'Ray'
I stare at the digits, recognize the area code as one in Florida.
I picture Ray catching marlins on a dock, a wide smile, large muscles, a beer and a
    cigarette near by.

I visualize Ray being easy, like Matthew McConaughey
A thick southern drawl like my father.

I imagine everything with Ray being relaxed and easily gotten
I imagine calling him now, from the room,
Flying to see him next week,

I copy the number into the back of the Didion book I have brought with me

I think maybe I will text Ray when I am back at home
I consider entering his number with your name, tricking myself into believing you've
    become the man I always wanted you to be.

WHITE PPL ARE LOOKING AT U

I hate when J. refers to you as 'Martin'
"I don't know any 'Martins' in alt lit," I say.
"Martin is not even an Italian name," I say.

Misery

In January my #1 fan came to town
I invited him to our house

"You have everything you could ever want here," my #1 fan said
He was looking around the house, looking at me
He was talking to my husband

I knew what my husband was thinking
My husband was thinking of *you* or of me *thinking of you*
My husband was thinking my #1 fan didn't know shit about what my husband had (or
    didn't have).

My #1 fan looked a little like Ryan Gosling if Ryan Gosling was someone you could
    overlook in a group setting; say, at a bookstore reading or something

My #1 fan was good at table tennis
After he left the rest of us joked he was still somewhere in the house
We pretended to be scared because being scared is fun if it's something you are only
    pretending to be

It is the same with jealousy
It is only fun in the abstract, I mean

Then again, it was sort of anticlimactic when we realized he wasn't in the house; when
    there was nothing or no one to fear

We all went to bed early after that

I Am Afraid to Leave My Hotel Room

I feel insecure about knowing which direction the vending machines are

I stare at a map on the back of my hotel room door

I remember before I left the house you said, "a real writer doesn't have to leave his/her
    normal environment to write"
you added a "wink" to your text to soften the . . .

currently I just want a bag of potato chips

it's funny how quickly isolation begets isolation

how hard it is currently for me to feel ok with being seen by the family at the pool which
    I would have to pass in order to get to the vending machines so I can buy a bag of
    potato chips

I can't believe you ever thought of me as a 'real writer'!

Ain't Nuthin' But a . . .

Finally at one in the morning I walked to the vending machines to buy a bag of fritos and
    a diet coke even tho I don't drink pop anymore

I wanted my life to be filled with fucking and Fritos and arcade games

I'd masturbated five times in a row that morning
I went back to my room and thought about watching porn but instead wrote this poem. I
    was thinking about Alanis Morissette. I was twenty-five when her song came out. the
    one about Uncle Jesse or uncle whoever.

And I'm here, to remind you, ~~of the mess you made~~.

I don't remember what else I was going to say after that.

[Add Here a Poem Abt How it's Not His Fault I'm Too Old to Bear His Child Now]

this will be the most painful poem in the collection

my stepdaughter has two boyfriends

and they both live with her in a trailer in —— , Michigan

E. says the *Twilight* books fucked her up; that she's never been the same since she read them in sixth grade

I think books and movies have fucked me up similarly

I haven't been the same since the year I saw *Henry & June* and *Barfly* back to back. I think it was 1989 but it might have been 1990. I want to live in a shitty apartment and eat corn raw from the field and get drunk and abusive with my shitty boyfriend (you?).

My stepdaughter lives in a canary yellow trailer with plants and candles and books on the occult inside and works at a store that sells

Pornos and sex toys

secretly I am jealous of her liberated lifestyle

For her birthday and xmas now I buy her three of everything: three tickets to a concert, three plates, three mugs, three saucers.

I think I am going to get a trailer in California or Texas or the panhandle of Florida and whoever shows up is okay with me.

NYE (2014)

I told you it was the worst new year's eve in years
Or maybe I said it was the saddest
I texted you this at eleven on new year's day
I set down my phone
I was used to you not texting back til three or four
I had a made up itinerary of your life in my head based on the small clues you gave me
    (some of which contradicted each other: "I don't drink" vs "the other night I blacked
    out at a blackhawks game" for instance.)

The night before I'd had a dream about Eminem but when you told me you had a dream
    about having sex with me I changed it to a dream about you so we could be the same
    or feel the same or something

I was tempted to say something to you like, "don't ever let me be w/out you on NYE
    again" but then I thought about what being with you on NYE would entail and I
    wondered if it was a case of being careful what you wish for

I wondered if what I really wanted was to be with Eminem but then I thought how even
    that might be a disaster

Poem titled 'self-fulfilling prophesy'

Alone inside marriage because I create that sitch in which I feel alone/ready for you

Algonquin Hotel, December 26th, 2014 (with daughter)

On the door of our hotel room is a quote from Dorothy Parker
Now I am thinking of the poem Dorothy wrote about waiting on a man to telephone her,
    while waiting on you to text me

I keep worrying I have no service inside this hotel room
But then a text from my husband comes through
disproving my theory about why you aren't texting me

Christmas Eve I was texting with Tanja while wrapping presents in my bedroom
I told Tanja you and I were texting again and Tanja told me about a friend of hers who
    goes to meetings for sex addiction

But I'm not having sex, I told Tanja
Doesn't matter, Tanja said

Sometime later I texted you, "I can't tell if we're in love or masochists or what"

"stop talking about your writing, butthole," you said.

And because there was nothing else to do but weep . . .

We have gone into Graham Greene territory
Entered into, I should say
This is a record of hate
I am entering lunacy, maybe
I am not well.
(this is my fondest self-quote)

I should like you to find me walking your city's alleyways
Barefooted through the snow
I should like to lose my fingers and toes
As some sort of Burroughsesque gesture to you
Van Gogh
To present them to you in a wrapped box

I should like you to be the one to accompany me to the emergency room
Jesus' Son
Then to a cheap motel where I won't know the day or month
Where we will grow disgusted and ugly and bored with one another

I lost all of my other poetry ideas when my old phone died

Raging Bull . . .

I think about cutting a line straight across your cheek or neck or other delicate places . . .

With your permission, of course—
providing the instrument,
watching in the bathroom mirror

Growing hard inside your umbros . . .

I am growing wet just thinking about it . . .

I always liked Angelina best when she was with Billy Bob.

I don't know how I like me best.

Postscript: *Friends* Is a TV Show from the '90s, Not Something You and I Will Ever Be; I'm Sorry

I have been masturbating more now that we are talking/not talking again.

I have masturbated more in the last two months than in the last four years.

I haven't told you this, of course, as part of my denying you (full) access to me and my thoughts.

But I am telling you here, now, publicly. HI.

Inner Rednecks, or, I Will Never Be Ugly Enough to Make Us Ugly Together

"ugly girls are the best," you say after I tell you I am tired of trying to be pretty

after that I send you a picture of me standing in front of my mirror in sweats and
    no makeup

I tell J what you said and she says, "he doesn't really mean that."

But I have already sent you the picture of me—
I am already ugly.

I wait for you to tell me I am the best.

I wait and six months go by and nothing changes.

Becky

I can't stop crying because I searched your name on twitter and saw that you sent a book
to a girl named Becky

Girl

I thought about changing 'girl' to 'woman' in the above poem for political reasons but then I thought changing 'girl' to 'woman' 'for political reasons' would be dishonest and pandering and we all know what I mean and every time I stop and think about something like that I think what happened to the punk movement, to the anarchy sign, which I hardly ever see anymore, and when did everyone I know start acting like the police while at the same time putting their babies in Ramones' onesies.

UNTITLed Unedited 'Liz Phair' Poem

Yesterday I listened to system of a down on repeat and today it's liz phair's supernova
I think this means . . .
Idk

I found a word doc called 'harry dean stanton' on my laptop I forgot abt
It was abt how harry dean Stanton asked a young actress he was working with on Paris,
    Texas why his character didn't talk and she said she didn't talk for a long period as a
    teenager because she was afraid if she opened her mouth she might . . . I forget

I wish I didn't talk sometimes
Like now
Like every time I open a Word Doc

Like, every time I spill my guts to 'you'

(j/k)

I am going to be yr good girl like I promised now as soon as I publish this novel
That's all abt you but not abt you at all I think yo8u will h8 it but I cannot control what
    you do or don't hate or I could have stopped you from hating me all those late nights
    and middays in which we raged in texts and said horrible things abt each other's
    writing/personas (lol)

I think listening to liz phair again is a good sign
(for me, I mean) not for anyone else (you?)

I am incapable of not pissing you off
Even tho I promise to be yr good girl
And I want to be yr good girl (I do ido ido)

(sorry, I had to stop to start Supernova over again)

what if I did tho
stop talking, I mean

to you
to everyone
stopped writing, I mean

who the fuck would care
it's not like I'm salinger here
it's not like . . .

I don't fucking know

I am typing standing up at my kitcen counter like I did ten years ago and it feels fucking
liberating and I urge eveyr young woman to write their bullshit poems abt men/
women like this

At any moment you can take two steps back and jump up and down like a pogo stick or
whatever

I would like to say a few words to my haters:

Instead I will just make a list of ppl who should never contact me again

markuginiadamrobinson   dylannicedelanynolan

(I don't need yrs or anyone else's permission or approval to publish this/idc if 'you'
like me)

I wish more ppl wrote shit that wasn't boring
(is this boring, baby? Tell me. I want to be yr good girl>)

I don't know how not to be defiant, I think
Esp when I have a keyboard in front of me

I guess that makes me a feminist
Or whatever

Everyone keeps talking abt molly soda and I keep thinking molly soda is a new soda
company like jones and looking for it at the grocery store when I can't sleep/write/
stop thinking abt how good I'm going to be for you

Now I am going to listen to the rest of the liz phair cd for you

I just realized you, Chelsea, and I are the only ppl I know w/out agents

Like wtf
Are we retarded or what

Remember when we were all on the train in 2009
And no one had an agent
And we all still wanted to fuck each other
And maybe read each other's shit (I think)

I stopped reading most ppl's writing in 2010 (I think)
After they got agents

I really like the first thing gene morgan posted on here

Oh, yesterday I listened to nirvana live too

I don't know why you need to know that other than that I think you need to know
    everything abt me

mira left half a joint here and I am going to smoke it alone tonight

Untitled (unedited) 'Liz Phair' poem 2

I wrote the above poem less than a week ago
I was feeling really manic (listening to system of a down and liz phair) because things
      seemed to be going so well ('for us')

I was standing a lot
Instead of sitting
I was smoking more cigarettes than normal and dancing and sweating

It's harder to write w/out thinking things thru when yr depressed instead of manic
I'm not trying to overthink this (poem/whatever); my mind is just moving so slowly it's
      impossible not to . . .

Currently not listening to any music
Currently feeling ready to not feel anything for a long while
While knowing I am incapable of not feeling anything
For more than two minutes at a time

I respond most favorably to acts of extreme (self-) humiliation and debasement

(duh!)

(pouty face)

my husband is in a hotel across town so I don't have to think about what an asshole I am rn

I don't understand what music goes with how I am feeling rn

I don't understand how one person uncomfortable with stability can help another person
      even more uncomfortable with the same

I think we could be a good couple if either of us could stop being insane for two pt five
      seconds, or, like 24 hrs or something

But then we wouldn't be 'us'! (smiley face)

But then we would hate ourselves/each other . . .

I would at least know what music to listen to then . . .

I think it's time to implement the harry dean Stanton/paris, texas phase of our 'relationship'

I don't know why I said I was a feminist

I think I am a thousand times more attractive silent

Did I mention today is my husband's birthday

Chelsea and Ian brought me two more joints from the weed mira left

I am going to smoke one wed night when I hopefully feel better abt myself

Or a lot worse

Either way

Last night after the conversation w my husband, I watched that salinger doc on Netflix

But it was so boring I ended up texting you against my will

I guess I will smoke a cigarette rn and listen to country music

I think it's funny when you in any way remind me of a country song

I like you best when you remind me of a country song, babe

When we were on the train I thought this was going to be forever

Maybe I wasn't wrong; this just isn't the way I envisioned forever would feel/be

Maybe this is better

Everyone else has paired off w ppl they respect and we just have each other's periods of great depression

Idk what I'm saying anymore

Chloe asked if I am having a manic phase and I immediately said no but maybe I am

I deleted yr contact info from my phone again

I'll probably reenter it at sum pt I guess (tonight)

This doesn't mean I don't respect you or you don't respect me or whtevr.

I think I am going to be ok w being alone now.

Untitled unedited poem 3

I guess I was lying when I wrote that first unedited poem almost a year ago

Remember how I sent it to a friend of ours to publish on his site and then I sent it to you immediately after that and you texted me at three in the morning, 'super pissed,' and didn't ask me not to publish it but basically implied I was a terrible human being for publishing a poem that was so current about us

It wasn't very feminist of me to get up from my bed where I had been sleeping to get on my computer and email our mutual friend to tell him I was no longer okay with him publishing it

I guess you proved I wasn't defiant when it came to you

I guess you proved I did care if 'you' liked me

I liked you because you were dominant and made me feel bad about myself

I liked feeling like a bad girl (for you) as much as I liked feeling like a good girl (for you)

The next day you texted me first which was highly unusual for you and I did not reply which was highly unusual for me

This was my way of trying to convince myself I hadn't been lying about being defiant (with regard to you)

I waited three days to reply to your texts (you texted me twice that day which felt like a huge 'win' for me at the time)

It was exciting having someone care so much about me that they yelled at me and told me I was a horrible person or insinuated that I was

I can't remember what you said exactly

That made me go immediately to my computer in the middle of the night to make things right

To make you see I wasn't a horrible person

To prove to you I was still your good girl
(even though you would never use that term to reference me again after that night)

I never understood why my husband didn't come out on the porch and yell at one or both of us the night you came to the party

We were outside talking for hours

My husband turned out the lights and went to bed (at some point)

Left me alone on the porch with you

You would never let me be that defiant.

But you're not here anymore anyway and my husband still is so I guess defiance isn't all it's cracked up to be or

Leonard Cohen Poem, or, I Wanted Always to Be Talking About Dead Rock Stars

My daughter called to tell me she'd just talked to her father. "He told me to tell you thank you for the Grateful Dead CDs. He was listening to one when he called. He said you don't need to keep sending him things. He said, 'Your mother likes to take care of people.'"

A few days earlier he'd left me a voicemail. At first I didn't know he was reciting a poem from the Leonard Cohen book I sent him. I just thought he was drunk at one in the afternoon again. He hasn't had a job in a couple of years. Last time I saw him he said he'd rather live on the street than wash someone else's dishes again. He started working fulltime at sixteen when he got his high school girlfriend pregnant. He had to use a fake I.D. to manage one of those Little Caesars they had in Kmarts at the time. He is turning forty in three months. I nodded my head when he told me that. I didn't blame him. There is a cherry tree in my front yard he planted for me four Mother's Days after we divorced. I never thought it would be so big. I thought it would die within a year. I guess I didn't appreciate it at the time.

I don't remember
lighting this cigarette
and I don't remember
if I'm here alone
or waiting for someone

He read with a slow determined voice into my voicemail. It was the same voice he used when drunk. He may have been drunk also. But I felt better after I knew it was a poem he was reciting rather than something he was telling me. But maybe they are the same thing anyway.

He was the age our daughter is now when I married him.

A couple weeks later he ran from me at a gas station somewhere in Minnesota or Wisconsin, I forget which. I didn't see him the rest of the night. I got a hotel room and waited for him to find me, which he did in the morning, when he was sober or not as drunk as he'd been at the gas station. I held him against my stomach all morning and then we kept driving west.

"I can't stop crying" is something you can only tell another person once.

"I can't stop crying" is something you write into a poem to give yourself a fifteen minute reprieve from crying.

"I want you to choke to death on my vomit," I said.
We were discussing the deaths of rock stars: Keith Moon, Janis Joplin, Hendrix, Winehouse . . . all the obvious ones.

You had mistakenly attributed Keith's death to choking on vomit.

I said, "I think you are confusing his death with John Bonham's."

Though I think I spelled Bonham wrong at the time. (Bonam, maybe. Or Bonnam.)

I said, "I think Keith Moon died in a swimming pool."

"No," you said.

"Vomit," you said.

"I don't think so," I said.

"I'm looking it up right now," you said.

It was our most 'normal' conversation to date. It felt like we were friends.

I pictured you at your desk (?) or sitting on your mattress with your laptop and phone. I liked picturing you alternating between your phone (me!) and your laptop. I loved that I was the one you were having a 'normal' conversation with.

Usually when we talked it was a lot of either yelling about who had more power in our 'relationship' ("don't use the word 'power'," you would say after being the one to use the word power) or commiserating on how tragic it was we weren't together with me not understanding why we couldn't be together and you knowing but not saying (you were the one with all the 'power').

I wanted to always be talking about dead rock stars with you from now on. I didn't want to talk about power or tragedy anymore. Dead rock stars would be our new common ground. When people asked us what we had in common we would say 'dead rock stars.'

"Drug overdose," you said, meaning Keith Moon. We were both wrong.

"How old?" I said. "Not 27," I said.

"I'm going to guess younger," I said.

"32," you said.

"Oh," I said. "How old was Bonham?"

I waited a few seconds while you looked it up. I loved the 'you' that looked up facts about dead rock stars on your computer for us. I wanted to always be talking to that you from now on.

"32 also," you said.

"Wow," I said. "A new club."

"I'm going to be 32 soon," you said.

"I know," I said.

"Remember," I said. "I'm 'obsessed with' you."

"I think I deserve it," you said.

I didn't tell you that two years ago I'd made the password on my computer your birthday. I didn't know if that was what you thought you deserved.

"Why do they always say 'choked to death on his own vomit'?" I said.

"Haha," you said.

"I want you to choke to death on my vomit," I said.

"32," I said. "The year you die," I said. "New club," I said.

"Haha," you said. "Yeah," you said.

We were both happy that night. Neither of us was talking about power or tragedy that night.

It's hard to pinpoint what went wrong this time just as it's always hard to pinpoint what goes wrong with us.

'I can't stop crying' is something you tell people over and over even though it makes them hate you because you have to tell someone and why not them.

Last night I watched a documentary about Sinatra and the narrator said all his songs were about loneliness and solitude. He said that with all Sinatra's fame and notoriety, he really just preferred to be alone.

My daughter's father hasn't dated anyone in thirteen years.

Maybe we can make a pact, you and I, to not date anyone for thirteen years.

(I'm sorry I am writing about things as they are happening again.
I don't know how not to write about things.)

You can only say 'I can't stop crying' once in a poem.

I'm sorry I keep saying it in here.

My daughter's father moved to a campground in Ohio last fall. It's spring now and pretty soon people are going to return to their campers and trailers. When we visited in March he was the only one there. He taught himself to play some Led Zeppelin songs on the guitar. He made us potatoes in the oven and played us the songs. I don't understand how he survives his loneliness. He said he let the classical radio station he donated money to in Flint know that he was moving to Ohio. He said their affiliate station gave him a shout out one night when he happened to be up at two in the morning. He said he rarely sleeps through the night. He rolls cigarettes and smokes them on the porch of the trailer. He said he is teaching himself some Nirvana songs too; that next time we visit he will play Nirvana songs for us.

Now when I think "Kurt Cobain" I think of your childhood lizard you killed instead of the dead rock star.

My daughter's father and I married two months after Kurt killed himself.

O.J. killed Nicole a month later.

My husband sat on my chest and bit my cheek because he thought I was cheating on him.

He pulled fistfuls of his hair from his head because he couldn't believe I loved him.

I think I have written that line before.

I am starting to repeat myself in everything I write.

I think of you sitting on my chest, biting my cheek, as a luxury I'll never have.

I think if you pull fistfuls of your hair from your head as a result of not believing I love you, you never tell me.

I think 'unfair.'

I just closed a letter to a young poet friend in Charlotte with, "I still don't know what I'm doing with 'my life.'"

I guess that's a good way to end this as well.

Middle aged white woman, or, My Miami Wkend w Gfs, or, George Harrison's Wife

There's a violence to your poetry now
When you lose everything you never really thought you'd have but are pissed you lost it
      anyway (I mean me here not you)

There's a violence to my thoughts now
That you have turned your back on me over a Miami wkend w gfs

I want to kill a bird for you with a handmade slingshot like a twelve yr old boy
Take a photo of it on my phone and text it to you, I mean
I want to be a twelve yr old boy for you if it means you will trust me and talk to me
Like a twelve yr old boy instead of a middle aged white woman

(typing 'middle aged white woman' is the hardest thing I've ever had to type/say to you)

I want my face to forever be covered by my hands so I never have to see you haven't texted
      me/so you never have to see I am a middle aged white woman.

I keep taking my wedding ring off and putting it back on depending on where I am going
      and who I might see

Which makes me feel like a fake or a phony
Two things you have accused me of being, recently

Maybe it's time to be asexual like Bruce Jenner so I won't have to make any more bad
      decisions

Last night my husband said the words 'I want a divorce'
We were walking to my car after dinner
I was wearing my wedding ring
I am nothing if not a fake and a phony!

I want to push a lawnmower until I collapse as a way of avoiding dealing with my feelings
      in the same way Eric Clapton developed a heroin habit because George Harrison's
      wife wouldn't leave George Harrison

Later, of course, after he'd written the song I refuse here to mention,
She did leave George Harrison.

But eventually that relationship busted up, too.

Is the saddest thing abt this poem the fact that I never named George Harrison's wife?
Or is the saddest thing abt this poem that I'll never be a twelve year old boy?

I Wrote This Poem on my tumblr in 'early 2013'

I am tired of writing sentences that begin "the woman."

I have come to the realization I now have more in common with aging, white,
    homosexual male writers than any other kind (you).

I have begun reading Edmund White almost exclusively.

I know more about you than any female you will ever talk to online or in person.
    (stop trying)

Any day now I will take to my bed like the aging debutante I remember reading about in a
    biography at my grandmother's house when I was eleven.

The debutante had been on the cover of *Life* magazine at age sixteen and photographed by
    Diane Arbus at age forty-five and you cannot believe the difference thirty years can
    make in the life of someone so irrelevant.

A bed fire feels almost necessary at the moment.

I wish Andy Warhol were alive to take our picture.

I wish I were as brave/self-destructive/ugly as Diane Arbus.

The only time I ever gave a shit enough to march for something was in Cincinnati in '89
    when they closed down the Mapplethorpe exhibit.

I sometimes think about having a sex change and then think about how I'd want to date
    young males if I did and then think what would be the point and the point would be
    gay culture.

I feel sufficiently isolated for gay culture.

I feel sufficiently criminalized for gay culture.

I would fist or fellate you in a bathroom stall, is what I am saying.

Inside a marriage is where a person can finally feel most subversive (and also most
    sadistic/masochistic—take your pick).

I think a lot about living at the bottom of a drained pool like Edie Sedgwick's character in *Ciao! Manhattan* but there aren't that many pools in the Midwest and I feel like you have to be fond of drugs to live at the bottom of a pool for an extended period of time and I'm just not that fond of drugs.

Given the chance, however, I will set this bed on fire!

I am the sort of person who can spend 24 hours a day in bed and chain smoke light cigarettes and drink coffee and bourbon.

I refuse to vote in any more elections until the taking of photographs of nude teenage males is legalized.

If you think taking drugs named for white, suburban girls is subversive, try again, faggit.

Mostly morality feels about as superfluous as religion to me at this point.

Mostly I consider myself amoral/asexual/apathetic.

When I hear someone say something about wanting to make the world a better place, I usually think this is about the person's need to validate him or her self and his/her inability to do so.

Mostly I feel like sex is stupid.

I am going to spend my last sixty thousand dollars living at the Chateau Marmont for an extended period of time.

Everything I write during this period will feel more important because it will fall under the title, *The Chateau Papers*.

After that, who cares.

After that I will probably end up stalking Dennis Cooper in Paris.

Nude teenage male bodies are beautiful and I want to hang them on my wall and view them in galleries, is all I'm saying.

Now that I am married, you never have to feel like you can't breathe again. (you're welcome)

I am already familiar with the depth of the pool at the Chateau Marmont.

Setting my bed on fire there, feels historical to me or something.

I want you to make a Wikipedia page for me and update it when this happens.

The photographs I take of nude teenage males at the Chateau will be something to march for.

I'm just kidding about the drugs. I think I will be happier taking them.

Homesick for Homelessness

Yesterday I was with my son at his university and my teeth did not bother me

(I have no memory of writing this poem)

Today I am home and my jaw hurts from self-inflicting and
Self-inflection and a characteristic inspection of self.

I am considering the seven p.m. showing of Scarface
As a way of killing three more hours this evening.

My husband is in classes and conferences all day.

Last night I dreamed of a friendship with Jennifer
Aniston, which I think must indicate or be indicative of . . .

My son told me over a lunch of crab cakes
And Thai shrimp salad that by the end of the semester
He will know more about the surface of Mars than almost anyone

I said, "Is it Mercury, Mars, Earth or the other way around?"

My son, who is actually a young woman, looked at me quizzically.
I assured her I was not joking.
(I can only remember that our dear Pluto is no longer a planet; perhaps
I am uninterested in remembering more—about our solar system or you . . . when did we
    all get downgraded to no longer being planets?)

It was good to see my daughter.
I sat beside her on a futon in her dorm room.
Her roommate came in and out and I wondered what it would
Be like to be her: the roommate, I mean. 'Mo-Mo'
Getting to know my daughter for the first time.

I'll admit: my knee-jerk response for dealing with
Things such as this (loneliness/isolation) is extramarital
Emotional affairs.

But I am trying to be someone else in this poem.

I have not replied to his/your latest email, which arrived, I must say,
In a very timely manner: the week we took my daughter to school.

(If I Google "perimenopause symptoms", does that make me a cliché?)
(menstrual cycles that arrive closer together, emotionality, greatly lessening or terrifyingly
    increasing sex drives, the want to drown oneself in a Beverly Hills bathtub . . .)

I am reading (writing?) poetry in the same tub Whitney Houston died in and my daughter
    is in the adjoining room.

I think I should have an actual affair in avoidance of insanity
Or suicide.

I am telling my in-laws this in a poetry magazine or journal
In case they are wondering my motivations for such
Atrocious behavior and consequences.

Their son is not a fan of my art.
Their son avoids insanity (and my art) with a nightly intake of whiskey and a porn
    collection that is the size and scope of the Internet.

My daughter already has one parent who suffers from mental illness,
Who has required hospitalizations and medications and diagnoses.

If someone must be hurt by my midlife crises, it cannot be her.

If you are struggling with your role as an 'artist', watch
Documentaries of Eugene O'Neill on your breaks.
No one ——s like Eugene.

"Homesick for homelessness," is a quote attributed to him.

As is: "I want to be an artist or nothing."

Have many more husbands must I exhaust (to save my sanity/to —— my art)?
I wonder now.

I remember All Good Boys Deserve Fudge but I forget the words (and their succession)
    that remind me the order of the planets in our dear & divine solar system.

I wonder: how does one be 'nothing' and will you be it with me if I reply to your email, 'at long last,' if I get out of this tub.

If not 'a planet,' what then?

This is what happens when a woman raised poor comes into $$$

I am shopping online in an effort to break my addiction to your blog.

I have a copy of *W* magazine on my lap and I am looking up every item from the biker chick spread.

I have so far bought two gold knuckle rings and a pair of leather pants.

Last night I studied the hair color of women my age and contrasted that with my hair color the year we met.

I am desperately trying to look younger for you so that you will still want me and I can refuse you.

I cannot bear the thought of being unable to refuse you.

I realized if I purchase this leather jacket and high heels and wear them to readings in nyc and philadelphia and d.c., someone will take my picture and put it on the internet and you will be forced to realize how much you hate the person I have become and wonder if this was the person I always was when you mistakenly fell in love with me (or whatever that was).

I am okay with you hating me as long as I am/remain foremost in your mind.

I am/will make myself the exact opposite of whatever you thought I was

I will make myself the epitome of everything you hate/represent

I will avoid eye contact with and spit near street punks with whom you identify and whom often look like you out of the corner of my eye as I pass them smugly, careful to hold my head high in the air as I would passing you now.

I will spit on you if I see you.

I will drag my six hundred dollar heel across your chest, dig it into your thigh.

I will tear a hole in the last pair of pants you own.

You will have to go to the salvation army every time I am in town!

The Internet Is Making Me Sad

I told my friend Scott McClanahan that on nights I can't sleep, I walk around my great-grandmother's house in Dayton in my mind.

The night before Scott had posted a video of himself dancing to 'Sweet Child O' Mine' on his Tumblr.

I didn't like thinking that Scott couldn't sleep.

My great-grandpa was nicknamed "Young" just liked Jay Z and had a glass eye on account of an accident in the factory where he worked.

I googled the address of my great-grandmother's house and sent Scott the link.

It made me sad to look at my computer screen.

I told Scott a secret in an email and then I didn't check my email for several days.
I hadn't cried in a long time and it was like a whole new experience.

When I was little my great-grandmother kept Tang in a glass pitcher in the fridge like the astronauts.

My great-grandmother had a swing in the basement we sat on because the porch was too small for a swing.

I don't ever want to Google Map the house I live in currently, once I'm gone.

I only want my heart to be broken in person from now on.

Cocaine Humor

Sometimes if I have more than one tab open on my computer it takes a while for my Word to close and I worry my husband will come up behind me and I won't be able to close it in time and he'll see that I'm writing about you again

Or maybe this is what I want to happen
I never know what I want

Natasha Lyon was asked by *Entertainment Weekly* for songs on her iPod and I listened to all of them but Lou Reed was the only one I downloaded

I just want to listen to the velvet underground and think about doing heroin even while knowing I never will

I want to read Andy Warhol's diaries again like I do every other year

Sometimes I find myself eating cheese puffs while staring blankly at a wall and thinking about ways to make you suffer

I find myself so bored without the pain you inflicted upon me or the pain I inflicted on you or myself or whatever

I had a dream in which I hated you and murdered you and fed little pieces of you to my dogs
But that wasn't a dream if a dream is something you have while asleep

I wanted to write that to you in an email, how much I hated you and wanted to murder you and feed pieces of your body to my dogs, but I didn't want to compromise my marriage so I resisted and wrote about it here in this poem where I'm allowed to talk to you

I wrote most of this poem in my head while walking the aforementioned dogs
With my husband

I read in the back of the bell jar last night that Sylvia Plath was conflicted about being both a wife and mother and a poet and writer

I have never read about any male writers feeling conflicted about being both husbands and writers

We passed a kitten on our walk or I saw one tonight on tv or something

Life is meaningless, and I mean that in a good way
The guy in 'of human bondage' came to the same conclusion
And then he went and got married in the last chapter anyway

I realized something tonight

Husbands and wives are only not boring when someone is cheating

Untitled dream poem, 2015

Last week I had a dream we were at a house party together
I kept walking through rooms looking for you
I found you on a couch in a room with other ppl
I sat down on the couch beside you
I tried to talk to you but you immediately made some sort of excuse
And left the room
I had the sense—in the dream—that this type of interaction kept repeating itself;
It felt like the saddest dream I had ever had

It felt like some sort of prophesy

Tanja was in the dream, too

This morning I ate too much Fiber One and read this manuscript up to this point and now I feel like I am going to throw up

I agree with my friend who urged me not to publish these poems
I agree with anyone who says these are not poems

'90s RIOT GRRRLS SONGS

(September, 2016–December, 2016)

Bluets

I finally tore *Bluets* in half @ 12:50 a.m.
I had had enough of it, of its blueness . . .
I had begun to loathe its preciousness, its precision
What it represents—
Its fans, the copycats
What it had made of women, female writers;
The academia, the polishedness, the politeness.
I missed the messy.
I loathed it for being a finished book,
Laid out and finalized in this form now in hand,
All its desisions made for it
I couldn't make one more desision
(I had forgotten momentarily how to spell "decision.")
I couldn't materialize an editor
(all editorial decisions had to be made by me!)
it was a blessing and a curse
(can you tell?!)

I had read earlier in the summer an interview with Grimes
She made being independent a record label or independent a producer
(I couldn't remember the precise ways in which Grimes was independent,
Only that it was important that she was.),
Sound enviable, fashionable, fun!

I found it to be a headache
I couldn't stop thinking of Grimes' ex boyfriend
The long car ride from Toronto to Montreal
In which he hadn't said a word
His current girlfriend, my friend, driving,
Myself and C and Tanja, muted by his intense
Sulking, in the backseat.

Later we watched a Grimes' video
In which he was featured.
His head was shaved then, too.

There is no one making editorial decisions here.
Oh, can you tell?

A Letter to My Daughter

for 'the infamous Barbara Jo'

I was raised in the '70s by a young woman who marched for Equal Rights, read books by Gloria Steinem (and other female intellectuals of the time), worked two jobs, owned a gun, shot guns, chopped trees, chopped a live turkey, snorted cocaine, snorted crank, drank men under the table, beat men at pool, beat men at cards, came undone for men and overshadowed men, who was arrested for physically assaulting her boyfriend and who was physically assaulted by him, who both hugely influenced me by introducing me to women like Anaïs Nin and Virginia Woolf and Alice Walker and Frances Farmer and Stevie Nicks and Colette, and who at times neglected me, leaving me for men, leaving me to work, leaving me because she was a young, restless woman in pursuit (a young woman who took responsibility for her actions)

The young woman—she was nineteen when she became pregnant with me in 1969, nineteen when she left my father who beat her, turned twenty shortly after I was born— wrote poetry also

I read these poems—kept in a thick manila envelope somewhere in her bedroom—when she was out of the house, working or at a bar with friends or with a man

And though they were never published, I read them and they meant something to me—

That my mother was a thinking and an engaged woman, apologetic and defiant, loved and heartbroken, self-accused and self-mythologized—

The young woman taught me, *above all*, to question everything, like Buddha, "even me (perhaps, *especially me*!)," and to take responsibility for myself (just as Joan Didion urges in her essays)

I'm not sure what I have taught you, what you will learn from my poems or from my writing, if you will even read it (I'd be just fine if you didn't!)

I think probably you have already taught me more than I will ever teach you, about not taking myself so seriously, about calling me on my shit, about a need to control my emotions, my adolescent heart

Remember that your grandmother and your great-grandmothers were each married and divorced three times, which speaks of a sort of defiant and independent spirit somewhere in our blood, or maybe of a bad luck in love, or of an intolerance of quiet unhappiness, a preference instead for out loud living, a penchant for hopefulness and self-reliance and resilience

My paternal grandmother said to me once, shortly after I gave birth to you, after a period in which she did not speak to me for a year, "I don't care if you're married or have a baby. Let me know when you finish college. Let me know when you have a career."

I didn't understand her then

I thought her cruel and unfeeling, unemotional, cold

I understand her worries for me now, her concerns (as you near the age I was then)

She wanted me to be financially independent from your father, which would ensure emotional independence as well

She was right; I had made my life harder

(It's hard to be both a mother and financially, and emotionally, independent)

My own mother paid a high price for her independence—working so many jobs I often felt abandoned by her

I did not view her working so many jobs as taking responsibility for herself, for her choices, until years later

I only thought she wanted to separate herself from me—and that work was one venue, and men another

This poem started out as a call to question and I suppose that is how it is ending

But in a different way than I intended

With me questioning the mythology I years ago created for my mother, and, by extension, for myself

I made myself the victim way more than I ought to have (in the stories I told people firstly and in my writing secondly), way more than was accurate, because I thought that was interesting, I believed that was where any interest in me lay

I did not view myself as interesting otherwise

Otherwise—without stories about my mother to define me—I was relatively boring and unappealing

Or so I thought

I am only now beginning to take responsibility for myself, for my own cowardice on the page and in real life

But how much is this, too, a show of sorts, how much can even this "revelation" be trusted?

I don't know

Is a writer ever to be believed?

Can a writer ever be trusted?

My only advice, dear daughter, do not become a writer

And this: never listen to your mother

Rachel Cusk Is An Intellectual So What Does That Make Me

I was reading a review of a new novel by one of my favorite authors
The author was female
A woman my age, slightly older
I had read a novel by the woman the year previous
It had been my favorite novel of the year
I had highlighted and quoted from the novel with enthusiasm and frequency

The review began by referring to the author as "a figure of some controversy"
The review talked about the author's first book—a memoir about being a mother
The review talked about the author "sacrificing her sense of self for her offspring"
The review referred to the author's "unapologetically intellectual perspective" on
mothering

I wanted to relate to the author
I wanted an *unapologetically intellectual perspective*!
Like the author and other women I read who seemed to feel similarly about motherhood

But when I thought of motherhood I thought about how sacrificing my sense of self for
my daughter had liberated me from myself
Had relaxed and centered me
Had been mostly positives, so few negatives

I was one of those poor sorts you read about who loves mothering, who breastfeeds
"extendedly" and sleeps with her child and doesn't drink or smoke or consume caffeine
the first six years of her child's life, who enjoys reading children's books and playing on
the floor, who looks forward to going on outings out-of-doors, to bundling up, to farms
and zoos, and into the wood

I had no complaints about mothering aside from the fact that having no complaints
meant I was not an intellectual

Or particularly interesting to talk to (on the subject)

Aside from the fact that having no complaints made me boring and unthinking and old
fashioned and unrelatable and simple

I had not been a writer when I became a mother

I did not feel I had anything to 'give up' in the early years of my daughter's life

I was gaining: companionship, rebirth, love . . .

I was being taught: patience and kindness, the names of the of dinosaurs, the types of big cats around the world, how to build a birdhouse, how to play Harry Potter, how to navigate my husband's schizophrenia in a manner that didn't completely disrupt my daughter's day to day life but didn't shield her from his world either, how to separate she and I from him when it was necessary, how to integrate him back into our lives when it was healthy to do so, how to raise a daughter, how to raise a feminist/scientist/strong woman/weak woman/heartbreaking and heartbroken woman, how to raise my best friend, how to be a mother.

The hardest thing to learn was how to let go (this is the hardest thing I have had to learn in life in general)

I still don't know how to let go (of anyone)

I still don't know how to talk about my sense of self without sounding like a cliché

Say Anything

My daughter and I were visiting my step-grandmother in Texas
My grandmother was living with my stepfather's second wife and teenage daughter in a
large brick house in Dallas

We were playing a game called Say Anything in my grandma's living room, which was
separated by a long hallway from the rest of the house

My daughter was seventeen, eighteen

My daughter was bisexual, queer, but my grandma didn't know this

I was leaving this up to my daughter to tell

We were seated in a circle in hardback chairs and my grandmother was in her recliner

The object of the game was to choose the answer that best fit the question-asker's opinions
so the question-asker would choose your answer

It was my grandmother's turn to ask a question

She chose a card

She chose a question from four possible questions typed out on the card

The question my grandmother chose was, "what is the worst organization in the
United States?"

There were four of us writing answers

The four of us writing answers stared off at the walls while we thought

My grandmother was eighty-eight, eighty-nine; she had lived twenty years without
her husband

My grandmother signed every letter and card, "in Jesus's name"

My grandmother believed her sister wouldn't be in heaven because she signed her letters
"God bless" and didn't mention Jesus

My grandmother didn't think my daughter or I would be in heaven because we didn't believe in Jesus

My grandmother was the kindest person I had ever met

I had spent most of my childhood weekends at my grandparents' house in Ohio
For thirty years, I was their only grandchild (even though technically I was a step)

My grandmother and grandfather had followed my mother's car twenty miles home if she'd been drinking when she came to pick me up

My grandmother had played card games with me and made me homemade applesauce and read to me on the couch, my head in her lap

My grandmother had shown me how to hang laundry out back in the yard and taught me Bible stories on a large felt board in the basement and gotten down on the living room floor with me to play Noah's ark

I wanted to believe in Jesus for my grandmother's sake but I couldn't believe

I wrote, "Planned Parenthood" on my card and turned it upside down

I had been going to Planned Parenthood for birth control and examinations for twenty-five years

I had driven my daughter and my stepdaughter and my daughter's female friends to Planned Parenthood on numerous occasions over the last four or five years, made numerous donations on their behalves

I'd had two abortions, one at a Planned Parenthood in Cincinnati and one at another medical facility in Detroit

These were all things I didn't tell my grandmother

We passed our cards, face down, to the center of the table; watched as my grandmother picked them up and read each one of them aloud

"'Democrats', okay."

"'G.L.A.A.D.,' is that the gay organization?"

"'Planned Parenthood,' good."

"'Feminists.'"

My grandmother smiled

"I guess you know me pretty well," my grandmother said. My grandmother sort of giggled.

"I was torn between Planned Parenthood and a gay organization," my stepfather's second wife said.

My stepfather's second wife was fifty, with big, blond hair and Mary Kay cosmetics.

When I met her fifteen years earlier, she had a nude painting of Marilyn Monroe over her bed, a dog named Monroe.

Now she was born-again, drove a car with a license plate that read: G SUS.

"But in the end I went with the gay organization," my stepfather's second wife said.

"That's what I'm picking," my grandmother said.

"It's so hard to choose," she said. "But I think that's the one. I think they're the worst."

I looked across the circle at my daughter.

My daughter had written "Feminists" on her card.

I watched my daughter wipe her card with a cloth; now her card was blank.

Later, before bed, I watched my grandmother hug my daughter.

"You're such a sweet girl," my grandmother said.

"I could just wrap you up and keep you here with me," my grandmother said.

My daughter smiled; she didn't say anything.

Empathy Exams

I started doing yoga and at the end of every yoga session, as we were all lying with our eyes closed, blissed out in corpse pose, the woman who led the class would invariably say something like,

"With each exhale of your body, let go anything that is not of love, that is not of truth. Breath by breath. Let it all go. Ask spirit that today you let go of all judgment, that instead you open your heart and you open your mind and you allow yourself to embrace not only yourself but all beings everywhere, and that you ask from the bottom of your heart, for peace"

I began to think about that, about truly opening my heart and mind, about asking from the bottom of my heart for peace

A lot of people I knew seemed keen on empathy for some people, for Muslims and women and minorities but not so keen on empathy for others, for Trump supporters and rednecks and young men in fraternities

I didn't know how you could have empathy for one and not another

For Muslims and not Christians or Mormons or Scientologists

For Democrats and not Republicans or Libertarians or Independents

For young women and not young men

I kept thinking of Dylan's song, "A Pawn in the Game"

My husband and I went to a zoo in Ohio

A lot of towns in Ohio were like my hometown: the factories were closed and there were few job opportunities and heroin was commonplace

Earlier in the summer my best friend's niece had died of an overdose

We'd stood in a circle in her parents' yard surrounded by cornfields and wood and tall grasses

Her father had worked thirty years at a factory making car parts and now that factory was closed

Most of the families at the zoo looked poor or working class, like their children would qualify as "my kids" for a Roger Waters' sing-along on stage

I remembered buying an annual zoo membership when my child was young because we had one car and not much money and it was a one time investment in a family activity we could do all year round

There were a lot of Trump signs on the way to and from the zoo and I felt no emotion staring at them; I felt neither positive nor negative, merely aware

I had recently found myself at dinner with a large group of people I didn't know or I knew two of the ten people

The conversation went like this, "I wouldn't be friends with anyone who supports Trump" and "can you believe [so-and-so rock star] is a Republican?" and "our neighbor has a big Trump sign in her yard and I know it's basically a big 'fuck you'"

I sat silently wondering when "a big fuck you" had become a bad thing

Or how they would know if someone had voted for Trump

I wasn't sure they understood that voting was private

I wondered if they thought everyone who voted Trump would be wearing a "T" on their chest the next day

I wasn't going to vote for Trump but I would be interested to listen to someone who was

I wouldn't not be friends with someone because she did

I wondered when people I knew who had been into the punk scene and owned shirts promoting anarchy had become against demolishing the system; why they cared

I thought the fact that a political sign in someone's yard was viewed as "a big fuck you" By someone who still owned a shirt with a big red A on the front of it was funny

I was amused that the person who thought it was "a big fuck you" had called to complain about it to someone whose job it was to field complaints about the size and number of lawn signs

The same way I was amused when friends of mine who made a big show about hating "pigs" were the ones who called the cops if an unleashed dog jumped on them or a neighbor mowed her lawn after nine pm

I yearned for a true anarchist

Or at least for the '70s when—NO MATTER WHAT HAPPENED—the worst thing you could do was call the cops

"I don't want the police here for any reason, got it?" my mother had said when a cop came around after my friends and I played ding-dong-ditch on an elderly neighbor when we were in the seventh grade

I never got the cops called on me again

I was more afraid of my mother than the police

My mother was Tony Soprano before there was a Tony Soprano, you dig?

Deer Widows Weekend

My mother had this friend Charlie

Charlie came from the wealthiest family in town but Charlie had disavowed his family or
　　his wealth or both

I first became acquainted with the word "eccentric" as it was used by my mother to
　　describe her friend, Charlie

Charlie was in love with an Amish woman
Charlie got his clothes from the Salvation Army
Charlie didn't go to college
Charlie worked at a dairy farm because he didn't go to college and didn't want his
　　parents' money

Charlie was a decade younger than my mother
I couldn't discern the make up of my mother's relationship with Charlie
My mother, on occasion, slept with Charlie's older brother Martin
Martin had gone to at least two universities in the Northeast and was a scientist in
　　Washington D.C. and only came back to our town every other year or so

I first became acquainted with the word "intellectual" with regard to Martin

I liked Martin, too
He was exactly between my age and my mother's
So I (very naively) thought I had a chance

Martin was charming

I couldn't tell what Charlie was

Once, my mother and I were at a bar with Charlie and Charlie paid a couple dollars
To buy me a fake rose from some lady
I remember its petals felt like velvet and it had an artificial rose-like scent

I didn't know what it meant that Charlie had bought me this rose

I was twelve or thirteen or fourteen

I didn't know how old the Amish girl was Charlie was in love with

A few weeks later I was home alone at night when I noticed a car parked in our driveway

Our driveway was long and tree lined

It took me a good five minutes to walk to the end of the drive to meet the bus in
the mornings

In summer you couldn't see our house from the road

My mother was bartending nights at a bar in town

We lived alone in an old four bedroom rented farmhouse

I called my mother at work to tell her there was a strange car parked in our driveway

By the time I worked up the nerve to call it had been parked there a good ten minutes,
maybe longer

I didn't call the police

My mother didn't call the police

My mother called my former stepfather, Wolfie, and his friend, Hog

Five minutes later Woflie and Hog were in our driveway, one on either side of the car

My mother told me later it was Charlie

He claimed not to have known anyone was home

My mother told me Wolfie and Hog told him he better get going, get out of here, and not
come back that night

My mother said there had been some sort of threat of violence also

That was the way altercations were handled then

KILL YOUR TV

Was a popular bumper sticker in the '80s and '90s.

I bought one and stuck it to the side of my 20" in 1994

I want to make a bumper sticker that says KILL YOUR LAPTOP so millennials will buy it and stick it to the outside of their laptops

And we can all feel better abt ourselves again

Chinese Restaurant

I was at a Chinese restaurant with a woman who had admitted associating herself with me was problematic. She said, "My students told me you're controversial."

One way to look at it was to be flattered her students knew who I was

I'd met the woman at the Chinese restaurant after a yoga class I was supposed to attend but didn't because I was (unexpectedly) depressed.

"I can't get out of bed," I had texted the woman two hours earlier. I was being my usual dramatic self.

"How was yoga?" I asked as she sat down across from me in the booth.

"I don't want to talk about yoga," she said.

I paused, unsure if yoga was somehow an unfeminist thing to talk about now.

"I want to talk about you," she said.

"Oh," I said, understanding, finally. She was being empathetic. She was expressing concern because I'd said I was depressed. "I should clarify," I said. "I wasn't in bed all day. I got up and wrote in the morning. Then I came down to eat lunch and that's when I got back in bed and didn't get out."

"Uh huh," she said.

"I have a hard time letting go of people," I said. I was thinking of the tortoises at the animal sanctuary.

"I just saw my daughter's ex's little brother," I said. "We had dinner with him two nights ago."

I remembered how earlier in the summer, during a phone conversation with the woman about my blacklisting, I'd been crying and she'd said, "I thought you were a tough, strong woman. You told me years ago you have to have a thick skin if you're going to be a writer."

I sort of remembered saying that. I'd edited and published her first story a decade earlier. Since then she'd gone on to win major awards, to attend parties at *The Paris Review* at which people like Salman Rushdie requested her presence. This is what she'd told me.

She said, "The other day Colson Whitehead retweeted me."

I was suddenly having a hard time getting a story published by a rinky dink online journal that three years earlier had jumped on a story I sent them.

I wasn't envious of her writing but I was envious of the ease with which she got it published, the frequency with which she was asked to fly to other cities to read and make (paid) appearances.

Earlier in the summer I'd taken three young female writers over to her house and she'd led us in a flower-gathering expedition around her neighborhood. Later we'd sat around a picnic bench in her backyard, smoking weed and making flower crowns. Mine was the worst one. I was no good at arts and crafts. She came over and made amendments to my crown, pinned it carefully to my head.

I think both of us were aware this was a love/hate relationship. Or that there were things about each other we found problematic but things about each other we were drawn to.

I was drawn to her fierce charisma and to her inability to edit what came out of her mouth, or her unwillingness to do so.

I wanted her to write the way she talked.

With the same fearless abandon.

To be fair, she probably thought I didn't take my writing seriously enough, didn't work it hard enough. I didn't give a shit about craft.

"I think you should go back to the animal sanctuary," she said. "It sounds like it means a lot to you."

It did but I didn't see a way to go back.

"Hey," she said. "Have you ever tried to wean yourself off antidepressants?"

"No," I said. "I've never taken them."

"Wow," she said. "You're the only person I know who hasn't. I'm trying to wean myself off mine before I take acid."

She had told me about this writing project, about a magazine I'd heard of but never read providing her with an expense account for LSD so she could write about some new trend of "micro-dosing."

"The idea is you take super small amounts so that you're never really tripping," she said.

It sounded like Hunter S. Thompson lite. I didn't understand the point.

I'd done acid twice.

I didn't recommend it

The other reason I didn't make it to yoga was because whenever I'm depressed or hung over, I end up feeling aroused

My husband and her husband had arranged a tennis match earlier in the day.

While I was in bed, depressed, I was reading this true crime book about a group of teenagers killing one of their own. But the book was mostly about the prostituting the teenage girls did and the steroids and porn the teen boys did. I should probably be embarrassed to say, reading about all that teen sex made me really horny.

I texted my husband to stop by the house before going back to his apartment.

"But I'm all sweaty," he said.

"That's okay," I said. He didn't get it.

He came into the bedroom and took off his clothes.

He was right: he was sweaty!

He got in bed and I read him the part I'd been reading earlier when I texted him. It was about some middle aged asshole white guy who fucked a girl he thought was fourteen but who was actually seventeen.

Actually he didn't fuck her, according to the true crime book he ate her pussy.

By now my husband was hard and I first fellated and then climbed on top of him.

I liked that he stank.

I had just finished my period but I guess having sex had brought it back. After, there was blood all over the sheets.
We had to strip the bed.
I had to scrub the mattress, soak the sheets.

I had to shower and by then the yoga class had started.

I didn't mention all this to the woman at the Chinese restaurant.

A long time ago she'd had a crush on my husband. This was another part of our love/hate relationship.

Hers and mine, I mean.

So I didn't mention it.

Sex Offender

Never forget: George Saunders met his wife in a creative writing class
When speaking about male privilege, I mean
When saint hooding George Saunders, I'm talking about

Close Encounters/Cunnilingus

My daughter and I were at the zoo
My daughter was twenty and an integrative biology major
We were standing in front of the gorilla yard
A male and female gorilla were hanging out near the glass wall that separated us
The female was lying on her back in the grass
We were standing on concrete
There were a handful of people, families, watching along with us

The gorilla offspring—two adolescent males—were playing with a cardboard box
deeperinto the yard

"Suddenly," or what seemed sudden to us and our fellow human observers, the male
gorilla bent down between the female gorilla's legs

"Oh," was the consensus of the human onlookers

Most took a step back and then another step in retreat

My daughter and I stayed planted on the concrete, our noses to the glass

The others had small children
There was the nonverbal consensus agreement amongst them this was something the
children shouldn't see

I had witnessed similar parental judgments at zoos, once when dead rabbits were thrown
to large carnivorous birds and once when an orangutan had spent a good three or four
minutes removing buggers from her nostrils with her finger and eating them off of it, all
while holding her young toddler

But the parents had not yet walked completely away either
They were curious like we were what might happen next

The male gorilla had first made what it appeared was a visual assessment of the female's
genitalia, then used his digits to spread her labia, and was now tasting her

The female lay still
I can't remember if her eyes were opened or closed

Something about the tasting had alerted the two young males
One began to stroll over first and the other followed

They stood on either side of their mother, watching their father's movements

They bent down closer, until their faces were on the same level as his, until only an inch or two separated them

They stared at their mother's open vagina and then one by one, they put their mouths to it as their father had, their father having stepped aside, one can only conclude, purposefully

This all occurred within a matter of seconds, maybe a full minute

And then the father strolled off and the boys returned to their cardboard box

The mother sat up, picking at some grass, fingered a stick

They were each of them very nonchalant about what had just taken place

And what had, my daughter and I wondered

A nonjudgmental exploration—visual and sensual—of a female's sex organ?

A teaching moment for a father and his sons?

"What were they doing?" we heard a child ask a parent

"Nothing," the parent replied. "Just playing."

We didn't hear anyone use the word "vagina"

I think I was twenty, twenty-five years old when I first heard the word "labia" used in a sentence

JEAN

I was introduced to my first gay couples when I was six by my paternal grandmother Jean who was a Republican and who had been married and divorced three times (the last time to a guy she referred to as "Fat Ed" when she referred to him at all, which was rarely; Fat Ed was an oil man from Oklahoma she'd met playing tournament bridge in Monaco or Switzerland, I forget which). She never married again. Uncle Tony and Uncle Elmo had a beagle named Snoopy and Aunt Margaret and Aunt Jane had a Westie named Misty and both couples lived in the same condominium as my grandmother in Clearwater, Florida in 1976. We had dinners at Tony's and Elmo's and sometimes I was allowed to walk Misty down to the pier by myself after dinner while the grown ups talked over cocktails. When we went swimming in the condominium pool we had to wear plastic bathing caps. My grandmother's had a plastic flower on the side of it and mine was unadorned. My grandmother had short hair and wore pants and no makeup and wanted me to have short hair and to play tennis. Most of my grandmother's friends were gay or lesbian and she warned me against being a lesbian because she said it wasn't easy, she said it was a harder life. She often remarked she wished she'd been born a man, like her younger brother, who learned how to fly and owned several small planes. I feel like I've written about this somewhere before but I can't remember where. Once, when I was in college, my roommate and I were visiting my grandmother in Florida and my grandmother flashed my roommate her crotch. To be fair, my roommate was a fashion design major and my grandmother was showing off her Bob Mackie gown. "She wasn't wearing any underwear," my roommate said. My grandmother was drinking a gin martini and laughing. We weren't allowed to go barefoot in her condo because she had white carpet and she said the oils from our feet would stain it. "She was wearing pantyhose, though, right?" I said.

Art Fair

I was walking through the art fair with Tanja

Half a million people came every year

I'd been going for a decade; it was always the hottest week of summer

Tanja had gone to art school in California

She wasn't impressed with the paintings of dogs in martini glasses,

The photographs of athletic stadiums

I said, "Come on, we'll walk down Liberty, that's where all the nonprofit and political organizations are"

"I want to see the greyhounds," I said

We turned up Liberty

We passed the Democratic Party and the Libertarian Party and the Young Republicans

We passed The Humane Society and the Catholic Church and Intact America, the anti-circumcision society

There was a Planned Parenthood booth on our left and right across the street on our right was a booth for Right to Life

An old woman was standing in front of the Right to Life booth holding a sign that said, "Women regret abortions"

 I wondered how she knew

I remembered those signs from the early '90s when I'd had my abortions

I kept waiting to regret my decisions but I never had

"I never regretted either of my abortions," I said to the woman as we passed

For a second the old woman looked a little startled

I thought about telling her regret and guilt and shame have to be taught, that they are never inherent, but Tanja was already a booth ahead and it was so hot and I wanted to pet the greyhounds

Chris Brown II

I was in Vegas watching a music awards show with three friends

Nicki Minaj was performing a song with Rick Ross and DJ Khaled

I said, "Chris Brown sings on this song too but I guess he couldn't make it tonight"

One of my friends said, "Why would anyone work with Chris Brown now?"

I had a lot of answers to that question but I realized quickly it was a rhetorical question, that my friend wasn't seeking an answer

I didn't run off crying into the other room, I mean

I guess maybe I had matured

The Ethicist

I was reading "The Ethicist" column in the Sunday *New York Times*

A man had written in to ask if he could tell the mother of an ex girlfriend that his ex girlfriend, to his knowledge, was now engaged in sex work

The man specified the sex work as found via a dating site for older men looking for younger women and that his ex girlfriend was "basically, exchanging herself for money"

The Ethicist answered that it was not the man's place to step in and that his ex was likely aware any risks and that the risks were to the man paying for the services also (and The Ethicist sited robberies of octogenarians as an example)

The Ethicist did, however, make the statement that he thought "many 'sugar babies' in your circle will end up regretting what they're doing" which felt to me similar to the old woman at the art fair holding the sign saying "women regret abortions"

Women regret sex work!

Felt similar in that it felt shaming, judgmental, and wishful thinking

I was beginning to view the idea of ethics and morals in the same way I viewed religion which was as an attempt at controlling the behavior of other human beings, to order one's world, to 'feel safe' in the face of uncertainty and unknowingness

A few months earlier I'd emailed a question to The Ethicist and then very quickly forgotten I had written it

My question had pertained to someone else's behavior, much in the way the man's question was regarding his ex's behavior, but posed similarly in that I was *ostensibly* asking if I should do something or say something about what I viewed as *someone else's* unethical behavior

When I received an email from an assistant to The Ethicist three months after I'd written my question I was excited but in the way one is excited to hear back from an author one has followed or a musician

My question had become, for the most part, irrelevant by this time, but I played along, took the phone call from the assistant to verify the details covered in my initial question

I was eager to see my question in print, as though a story I had written or a poem was being published

I told my daughter and my husband and a handful of friends

I waited eagerly one week and then two

When finally my question (and The Ethicist's answer) was printed in the paper, however, I felt almost immediately regretful and ashamed that I had put in print the judgment I made on another human or small group of humans

For this was the real point, wasn't it?

Not so much the answer, which turned out to be as muddled and unclear and ambiguous as my own regarding the question, but the tsk-tsk'ing of the other person's behavior

Of the small group's behavior

Perhaps it is a form of irony that I did not regret either of my abortions, that the man's ex may never regret engaging in sex work, but that I regretted asking a question of The Ethicist that did not concern my own behavior but someone else's

Perhaps someone should make a sign

You Have to Believe in Sluts to be Slut-Shamed

Another friend of mine was attempting to have an open relationship with her husband

I was observant and curious
It seemed like a Catch-22 situation
Monogamy, I mean

I had never seen an open relationship turn out well
Though, to be fair, I wasn't sure I had ever seen a monogamous relationship turn out
    well either

You were either repressed or you broke up, divorced
My husband and I have broken up three times, maybe four
Depends on what you consider, "broken up"
My friend was telling me about a time recently she had finally put her "theoretical" open
    marriage into practice

She was vague on the details, saying only that she had been "caught" by her husband

When he caught her, she said he said, "You don't even seem to feel bad about it"
To which my friend replied, "Because I *don't* feel bad about it!"

I wanted to yell out, "Bravo!"
But we were in a restaurant
And part of me was worried my friend wanted to have sex with my husband.

I wouldn't have minded having sex with other people but I didn't want my husband
    having sex with my friend.

It was a Catch 22 situation,
Life.

I told my friend my problem with *Lemonade*, relating it to my friend's attempt at an open
    marriage. Relating it to her not feeling "bad" about what could be perceived as her
    infidelity. Relating it to what is perceived as Jay Z's having "cheated."

She said, "So you don't believe in monogamy?"

Which surprised me because it seemed like she didn't believe in monogamy, either.

I said, "I do, but you're going to be repressed."

My friend nodded her head.
We were in agreement.

You were screwed—or not screwed—either way.

Freaky Friday

I was showing my daughter one of my poems
It was one of the poems about her
She looked at it, holding the paper loosely in her hand, noncommittal

"I guess this is what passes for poetry now," she said, handing me back the paper

Literati

I was sitting on my bed reading when I saw on my phone that the man from the bookstore was calling

"Shit," I said. I was looking at my cat. "This can't be good news," I told him.

I didn't answer the call, not because I didn't want bad news, but because I almost never answer my phone.

A few seconds later, there was a text from the same man. The text said, "We need to talk."

I looked at the cat. "Fuck," I told him. "This news is getting worse by the second."

I picked up my phone. "Okay," I texted back.

My phone rang. It was a week until the reading we had scheduled at the bookstore was to take place. We had scheduled the reading months in advance. The man at the bookstore had said, "I know [your author] is controversial but I would never not sell his book in the store, I would never not have him read here. If we did that, we'd have to pull the books of Anne Sexton and Oscar Wilde and Sartre and de Beauvoir and Bukowski and David Foster Wallace and T. S. Eliot and a thousand others."

Now the same man was saying, "Look, I'm sorry. But we're going to have to cancel the event. There have been complaints. Someone has said they don't feel safe with [your author] in the store."

I didn't know what to say so I said, "okay."

I said okay and hung up the phone. It was time to get ready for my job volunteering at the therapeutic riding center. I had to put on jeans and boots and a long underwear shirt. I walked beside three different horses holding onto the legs of three different children and then I was back home again.

I dragged the garbage canisters to the curb because it was trash day in the morning.

I sat on my bed, looking at my cat.

]my author] and three other writers had bought tickets to fly in for a reading that wasn't going to take place in six days.

[our author] had been accused the year before of having sex with a minor when he was 22 and the young woman in question was 17. My daughter and her boyfriend had been 15 and 19 when they started dating and they'd been dating for five years.

The national drinking age had been raised to twenty-one when I was a teenager.

The graduating class ahead of us had been grandfathered in, meaning they could still buy beer and wine at the age of nineteen.

We were the first class who drank illegally, at age nineteen, under the new law.

I didn't think there was anything immoral about drinking alcohol before the age of twenty-one, even though it was technically against the law now.

I didn't think I was incapable of consenting to sex at age seventeen years and eleven months and twenty-nine days and suddenly capable of consenting the day I turned eighteen.

I didn't look to laws and lawmakers to tell me what was moral or ethical or 'right,' given the history of laws and lawmakers in this country and others.

I couldn't think of anyone who hadn't smoked marijuana, for instance, despite it's illicitness. I'd had two abortions and sometimes in history abortions were legal and sometimes they weren't.

I thought most people were full of shit, is what I'm trying to say.

The ones who now clung to laws and lawmakers as guidelines for morality, anyway.

It was a witch hunt, is what I'm saying.

I went down into the basement to smoke a cigarette. Pretty soon they would be illegal too.

Literati II

Two days later my husband and I met the man from the bookstore at a bar next to the bookstore at his request

We had been friends with the man a long time

The owners of the bookstore, a married couple, came, too

We sat in one side of the booth, my husband and I, and across from us sat the man and the wife and the husband in that order

The husband didn't say much, kept his head down, hidden in the palm of his hand

Mostly the man we were friends with talked because the man we were friends with was the bookstore's events coordinator

The wife sat very erect and stiff with her head held high and her gaze straight ahead at us, unblinking

Occasionally she would say, "It's just business. It's a business decision."

I had avoided speaking with the wife over the years

Since the bookstore had opened two years earlier, the husband and wife had spoken almost exclusively with my husband

The day the bookstore opened they had made a prominent display of our books as their first monthly nod to local literature

I sat erect and stiff to mirror the wife

A song by Tom Petty played in my head

The man from the bookstore talked and my husband talked and the wife said, "We didn't know anything about it."

The man from the bookstore said, "We are trying to prevent a disruption—we have reason to believe the reading would be disrupted"

My husband and I said, "That's fine. We're fine with a disruption. We're fine with a protest. We welcome and encourage conversation and questions."

I could see the man from the bookstore didn't want a disruption; he didn't want conversation and questions

The wife repeated, "We didn't know anything about *all of this*"

The wife was effectively throwing the man from the bookstore—our friend—under the bus

The man from the bookstore looked like he hoped a bus would accidentally kill him

The wife said, "one of our best customers" and "university" and "safe"

The wife said, "Business. It's just business."

I said, "Fine, we have to pull all of our books then."

"It's just business," I said.

On the drive home, my husband and I each sent a text to the man from the bookstore

The man from the bookstore and my husband were supposed to go to a concert together that weekend; my husband and I were extending our continued friendship to the man

We said, "We hope this doesn't affect our friendship"
We said, "We aren't blaming you for this"

The man said, "I need time to clear my head."
The man said, "I need to take the weekend."

My husband and I waited the weekend and then waited the month and then waited a year.

We didn't hear back from the man at the bookstore.

We held the reading at our house.

The house was full of university students. University students filled our living room and spilled out onto our balcony. University students smoked weed and smoked cigarettes and bought books and asked [our author] to sign books.

A year later I was entering the party of a mutual friend. The man from the bookstore was on the balcony in conversation with someone. I had to pass in front of the man to enter the house. I passed the man without acknowledging him. I had given him a year.

I was empathetic but I was also Tony Soprano.

I was empathetic but don't push me.

Literati III

A man I had significantly helped during the first five years of his writing career and who had married my husband and me was reading at the bookstore that had canceled our reading the year prior

My husband and I found out via the local paper's listings

My husband had stayed at the man's house on a reading tour two months earlier

The man had not once come to town without first contacting my husband

The man had texted me the morning my essay went up two years before to offer me his support or to say it was well written, I can't remember which

That was before the huge backlash

I had not heard from the man since the huge backlash

The man cultivated a 'clean' social media presence
The man posted about jogging and dinners he made for his wife

I said to my husband, "I'm going to protest [the man's] reading. I'm going to hold a sign that says, 'I remember when this man read and loved every book by Dennis Cooper!'"

I said, "You can't read and love every book by Dennis Cooper and not have a dark side, and not be hiding something"

My husband couldn't get through the beginning of a Dennis Cooper novel (maybe my husband was hiding something!)

Once the trend had been to like Dennis Cooper novels, to admire the subversive, and now the trend was to appear as upright as possible.

The man had been nice to me when being nice to me was an advantage and now that being nice to me was problematic the man avoided me.

I'm not Tony Soprano but don't push me

Literati IV

I had a dream in which [our author] went to the bookstore the night of the reading anyway

Sat down in the middle of the floor
And we all sat around him
Our other authors and I

A peaceful protest

A sit-in

On the bookstore floor

Burning Down the (Author's) House

An author was being interviewed on the radio

The author was a woman who was known to have dated a male author who was now dead of a suicide

I waited the whole interview for the interviewer to ask the female author about the male author

I had heard this particular interviewer ask other guests about the male author previously

The female interviewer had evidenced an interest in suicides (that seemed separate from her interest in people)

It was like a game I was playing with myself, seeing how long it took her to ask/how she would bring it up

Finally, after enough time had passed to show an interest in the female author herself, the interviewer segued to talking about the female author's more famous boyfriend

"He asked you to marry him, didn't he?" the interviewer said.
"He had your name tattooed on his arm, isn't that right?"

The female author answered all the interviewer's questions patiently and politely.

Then the interviewer asked a question of the female author that seemed to test her patience. The female author said, "Look, I could burn [male author]'s house down if I wanted to, but I'm not going to."

I thought that was a funny way to say you weren't going to do something you'd just done

"Everyone who dated [famous male author] knew he was violent," the female author said.

Now I and everyone else listening, the interviewer included, was imagining things the male author might have done, a whole host of them, many of which were probably way worse than the actual things.

Or maybe they weren't.

Maybe [famous male author] is Chris Brown here
Maybe we should ban him too!

Not Punk

I was at the house of a writer
She and her husband were both writers, actually
She said, "Do you want a tour of the house?"
I said, "Sure," then the baby cried and she said, "It's a self-guided tour."

I went upstairs and began to walk around

I walked into an office stocked with books about the country of the husband's origin
The office was sterile and impersonal; not much to see

Across the hall was another office
Hanging on the wall was a shelf filled with crystals and rocks
There was a small bookshelf over the desk and I thought I saw my book on the shelf,
Though now that I am writing about it, I'm not so sure
Maybe I am only envisioning what I wanted to see

Anyway, on the wall beside the bookshelf was a sheet of paper with two side-by-side lists:

"NOT PUNK" and "PUNK"

On the "NOT PUNK" list was:

• blowjobs
• cocaine
• Arthur Miller
• New York City
• therapy
• Tupac
• Lydia Davis

on the "PUNK" list was:

• cunnilingus
• marijuana
• Marilyn Monroe
• the desert
• couples therapy
• Biggie
• Elizabeth Ellen

They were good lists; I was tempted to take a picture of the lists so that I would remember
   everything that was on them

So I wouldn't have to make up some of the items on the lists (as I've had to here)

But I didn't think taking a photograph of the lists would be very PUNK

I thought taking a photograph of the lists was decidedly NOT PUNK

So instead I tried to write about them from memory
Which may or may not be PUNK

I'm not sure

I'm pretty sure my book was on the shelf

(I'm pretty sure mentioning that is NOT PUNK)

University Town

My husband and I walked to a wine shop near our house
It was autumn and sunny and we wanted to drink
We walked around studying the different regions and types of wine for ten minutes, then
    picked a bottle because an image on the label
Appealed to my husband's sense of nostalgia

After we had chosen our wine we each ordered a hot tea
It was still early and I wanted to be wide awake for
When we started drinking
The tea took four minutes to steep so we sat at a table across from the register to wait

A man and his son were at the register purchasing bottles of some sort of beverages
The man said to the cashier, "You only have one non carbonated drink in your whole store."
The cashier said, "The wine isn't carbonated. Or the coffee."
The man said, "My son here can drink carbonation but my other son who isn't here
    doesn't like carbonation. What would you have for him to drink?"

My impulse was to help the cashier out by shouting, "water," but I hadn't yet had my tea,
    so I refrained.

The father looked old, like maybe he'd waited too long to have children.
If he'd had kids sooner, he probably wouldn't be asking about non carbonated beverages,
    I thought.
He'd probably have "more important" things on his mind, like how he was ever going to
    get laid again by someone other than his wife and how he and his wife were going to
    pay for groceries until his next paycheck.

He probably drives a Subaru, I thought.

What kind of punk ass white kid doesn't like carbonation, I wondered.

Maybe I was just sour because I hated the (non) taste of still water

No, I thought. Not liking carbonated beverages was something that's taught
By the same parents who put their babies in Ramones onesies
And tell you their two year old knows all the words to Jay Z *Unplugged*

Yin Yoga

I bought a yoga DVD at Barnes and Noble for half price

The DVD focused on yin yoga

All I knew about yin yoga was that it consisted of a series of floor poses held for five minutes each

It was supposed to be relaxing and to help you sleep

I liked yin yoga best of the classes I had taken but each of my three friends preferred the type of yoga that was hot and sweaty and burned calories

That type of yoga made me feel lightheaded and nauseous and like I was going to pass out

I bought the yin yoga DVD to do at home in the comfort of my office

I bought the DVD before Thanksgiving and then my in laws came and my daughter came home from college and I forgot about it

It was two weeks later, on a break from writing, that I found it again

I had been home alone for three days

Trying to finish these poems

My only interactions with other humans were the Bret Easton Ellis and Marc Maron podcasts

I put in the yoga DVD on my break

Warmed up my coffee

A man came on screen who bore a resemblance to my friend's husband

He didn't look like my idea of a yoga instructor, is what I mean

He looked like my idea of a friend's husband: bald and stocky and middle aged with a small gut and a gentle personality

Almost immediately, I felt soothed by his presence

He was standing before a large white board

He said he was going to give 'us' an introduction to yin yoga but in order to give us an introduction to yin yoga, he had to contrast yin yoga with yang yoga

I had not thought of yin yoga in regard to the yin/yang symbol I had seen on the silver rings and Mexican bajas I'd sold at the hippie store where I'd worked twenty years earlier

I'd never heard anyone refer to any yoga as 'yang yoga'

The man wrote 'yin' on one side of the board and 'yang' on the other

The man cautioned us about thinking in absolutes

The man said, "I am going to talk in absolutes but nothing is absolute"

The man said, "The stronger the statement, the less true it can be"

The man said, "When I talk in broad strokes it is to elicit in you a conscientious internal objection: 'no, that can't be completely right'; and that is good, that is what we want"

The man said, "It is easier, faster, to make big, bold black and white statements but it is very important not to get trapped in them."

The man said, "It is easier to speak—it is easier to communicate—but whenever I say something REALLY BIG and REALLY STRONG, there should always be creeping up in the back of your mind, 'That can't be absolutely right. That's too strong a statement to make.' And that's what we want."

I thought: AHA!

I thought: Yes!

I thought: QUESTION EVERYTHING!

I wondered if yoga was a cult and if I was being brainwashed into it

I checked the time on the "introduction to yin yoga"

It was two hours in length and of the two hours I had so far watched seven minutes and eighteen seconds

I took out the DVD marked "theory" and put in the DVD marked "practice"

There were two practices from which to choose—"spine" and "hip"—and I somewhat hesitantly and randomly chose the spine series

I sat upright and cross legged on the floor, waiting to begin

The man who looked like my friend's husband came back onto the screen

This time he was sitting elevated on a large block and four people were seated on the floor on either side of him—two men and two women

He began to lead us in a series of elongated floor stretches, each lasting four or five minutes, while he remained seated on the block, talking to us the entire time

It wasn't until we got to "snail pose"—"an upside down curling, rounding of the spine" that he referred to as "our climactic forward bend" and which would lead us then into backward bends, that I began to feel *uneasy*

I had watched my mother do "snail pose"—though I did not know at the time there was a name for it, it was merely my mother lying on her back on a braided rug in our living room and throwing her legs up over her head, resting her feet on the floor on either side her head for thirty seconds or a minute—throughout my childhood, and had copied it myself over the years, though never holding it as long as the man on the DVD was now asking me to hold it

"What's unique about yin yoga is we are attempting to pull your bones apart," the man was good naturedly and seemingly non-sadistically saying

"If you succeed, you should *momentarily, temporarily*, feel fragile and vulnerable"

I felt fragile *and* vulnerable and I didn't like feeling either

I kept sitting up every minute or so to take a break from feeling fragile and vulnerable

"Temporary fragility is a sign of success. It stimulates the body to rebuild that area of the body stronger and more elastic," the man said

I wondered if he was speaking in metaphors

I thought about all the others times in my life I had felt *temporary fragility*

After snail pose we moved on to simpler, less taxing positions for another twenty minutes until I heard the dreaded, "One last climactic spinal movement" which led us into "saddle pose"

In saddle pose you sit upright on your knees and then lower your head and back down onto the floor behind you, while your knees remain bent in front, your calves underneath you

I had watched my friend C. do it but had never attempted it myself

It looked simple enough when C. did it but I knew that was a trick, an optical illusion, which is why I had never myself tried it

"For modern peoples, this is where we're most afraid," the man was saying. "The lower spine and sacrum"

I didn't know if it was comforting or disconcerting, being told where I was most afraid

I slowly lowered my head backward toward the floor, stopping short of full surrender

"And it's scary and frightening for many people to try to put any stress into their sacrum and lower back. Fear and trepidation about this area of the body is pretty much universal in the classes I have taught."

The man was now chuckling to himself

I couldn't go any further

I didn't trust my own body not to get stuck down on the floor in this pose if I allowed it to go all the way

I no longer trusted this man not to be a cult leader

"A *momentary*, *temporary* feeling of fragility and vulnerability is exactly the effect you're trying to feel in your bones in these postures."

He kept repeating "momentary" and "temporary" in a long drawn out way that was meant to be reassuring but just seemed like how a cult leader or abusive boyfriend would get you to do something you didn't want to do

I sat upright in defiance

I thought, "The stronger the statement, the less true it can be"

I sat cross legged, mirroring the man

I waited to stop feeling fragile and vulnerable

It took a full minute

I was lucky

With a cult leader or an abusive boyfriend it could take a lot longer

I wasn't sure if somebody you follow on social media could be considered a cult leader but I thought it was worth pointing out here, the possibility

The stronger the statement, the less true it can be

Only Women Bleed (Bucket List)

We were in a restaurant in Miami Beach
It wasn't spring break but we were in Miami anyway
Four of us, like *Sex and the City*, but in Miami

I couldn't tell if I was the slutty one or the square one
We hadn't yet been to the strip club or tattoo parlor
These things would reveal themselves in time

Midway through dinner, another woman showed up
I'd met the woman before in another city—maybe one in Ohio,
But the woman sat by my friend and talked mostly to her—
Turned her back to the rest of us—
But in a loud voice so the rest of us could hear, so that it was awkward to talk while she
was talking

"And then, I don't know why, I wasn't wearing a tampon or a pad and I just sort of bled all
over the hotel bed," the woman was saying

"I'm bleeding all over myself right now," the woman said

The woman was eating a carrot dipped in hummus

The woman had short, cropped hair like the American woman in *Breathless*
And was wearing a long, floral dress and I imagined what was happening underneath of it

It had never occurred to me once in my life to not wear a tampon or a pad while
menstruating
and my immediate reaction was to feel horrified,
As though the woman had revealed she had shat in her bed and not cleaned it and slept in
it anyway

My reaction did not alter for almost two years
I was still always horrified when I thought of the woman willfully bleeding all over the
hotel bed and willfully bleeding throughout our Miami dinner

The woman had seemed, to me, crazy; out of touch with reality—
Eating carrots and hummus while bleeding on a restaurant chair

And then, just today, something shifted within me—perhaps it was all this anger I've been
complaining about—

Suddenly I was aware the liberation in the woman's unencumbered menstruation,
The freedom she had recouped in bleeding freely and openly and without shame,
Onto her nice floral dress and (presumably) her underwear

It was the last day of my menstrual cycle
(Every menstrual cycle counted now in a way they hadn't when I was younger!)
I put on a pair of cotton underwear and a pair of sweatpants and came upstairs to work
I worked for half an hour before I detected a slight dampness

I shifted in my chair and kept working

I was determined to feel free and liberated!

I told myself it was just a liquid like any other, nothing to worry about
I told myself to stop being a baby, to stop being so affected by societal norms

STOP BEING A GODDAMNED YUPPIE! I thought silently to myself but did not yell aloud

I worked and squirmed uncomfortably in my chair another half an hour
Every so often I raised my ass off the seat to check and always there was nothing under it

Finally I got up to go to the bathroom
I examined my underwear as I peed
It was reddish brown in the crotch
I stepped out of it on the bathroom floor
Carried it to the sink and began running water

I was the goddamn square washing my underwear out in the sink
Spraying the crotch with Shout and rubbing the fabric together briskly with two hands
The way my grandmother had shown me when I was twelve years old

When before there was blood there was a thick yellowish stain that dried to a thick
    yellowish crust—
A fine powder I could scrape at with my fingernail,
Flake across the bathroom,
Hold to my nose for observational purposes

I rinsed my underwear and sat back down on the toilet, shoved a tampon in

I added "menstruating in a hotel bed" to my bucket list

But I didn't have a bucket list so I wasn't ever going to menstruate in a hotel bed

Just as I was never going to do heroin

Just as I was never going to have sex with a woman with a strap-on

(Unless you're willing, I mean; unless you provide the strap-on)

Academia

My husband and I were invited to a party

I told the hostess I probably wouldn't go

"I don't feel comfortable around the faculty," I told her

"Don't be silly!" she said. "I'll make you a flower crown. You'll be fine."

My husband worked at the university

But he wasn't tenured

(The hostess was tenured, was the young star of the creative writing program)

I was blacklisted
I'd had a falling out with the bookstore in town where everyone read
It had severely cut down on socializing
I was used to staying home alone

My husband texted me from the party, "You should come! There's no one here. I'm just
    sitting out back with R—— and M——."

My husband had his own apartment

I was on my way to clean it

(I liked the smallness of my husband's apartment, my anonymity within it)

I was driving with a bucket filled with cleaning products on the front seat

I wasn't wearing makeup

I was wearing an old Guns N' Roses t-shirt

My hair was greasy

I was halfway to my husband's apartment

Two blocks from the party

When a song by Mötley Crüe came on the car radio

Something about the song was inspiring

Maybe it was the drums

I felt strangely emboldened

I stopped at the 7-11 on the corner,

Bought a Diet Sprite and a bag of Swedish Fish

I parked my car several houses up the street from the party

Watched people entering and exiting from the front seat of my car

The house reminded me of one in a Michael Chabon novel or an Edward Albee play

Or perhaps its inhabitants did (reminded me of characters in the same)

The Mötley Crüe song was long over

The 7-11 man had called me "hon"

I'd felt grateful rather than suspicious of the pet name

I'd felt strangely cherished, endeared

I felt naked strolling up the steps to the big front porch

I pretended otherwise, I feigned strength and coolness

I walked without hesitation through the house, down the back steps, into the yard

I did not hesitate when faced with the man from the bookstore who was in conversation
    on the back porch

I was Patricia Highsmith entering a literary party with a purse filled with slugs

What the hell did I care about a small man with a small mind?

I found my husband standing around the fire in the backyard with R—— and M—— just
    as he had said

"You tricked me!" I said. "You said there was no one here and there are a ton of people here and they're all from the university"

"I guess I didn't notice," my husband said, looking around

"And of course the first person I have to see is J- from the bookstore!"

"Yeah," my husband said. "He's here."

I had been talking rapidly, had not taken notice of my immediate surroundings

Behind my husband sat a poet from the university, seated on a log by himself

I had once had a mild acquaintanceship with the poet, before he was at the university, before I was blacklisted

Since then I had seen the poet several times at similar gatherings and each time we had pretended not to know one another and I wasn't sure if he did not want to know me or thought I did not want to know him

It was hard for me to trust anyone now

I wanted the poet to want to be my friend but I could not make myself that vulnerable

I was too easily hurt

I made eye contact with him and looked quickly away

An act of self-preservation

A knee jerk assumption that everyone now hated me

The hostess was nowhere in sight

I was not going to be made a flower crown

I was going to stand here for one hour feigning strength outwardly while collapsing inwardly

"I am never again coming to one of these parties," I told my husband

"Everyone from the university is so serious," I said. "I never see anyone laughing"

I watched the poet to see if he laughed

His office was right across from my husband's in the English building at the university

My husband had told me that the poet had recently peeked his head into my husband's office, waved a hand, said, "I just wanted to say 'hello!'"

My husband and the poet did not speak at the party

Why didn't anyone speak?

Everything about the party felt repressive
I could barely breathe

I shoved Swedish fish in my mouth as an opportunity to gulp air

I watched the poet's girlfriend—who was also a poet and also employed by the university —approach him

I watched to see if either of them laughed

I watched them leave the party together

I wanted to sneak around the side of the house, to spy on them in their car

I was desperate to know if they laughed when alone together

I needed to find out if somewhere underneath the prim and proper academic presentation, they were real human beings, after all

Real human beings who picked their noses alone in bathrooms and farted during sex;

Who laughed at the farting, who loved and were loved

Instead I stood awkwardly in the small circle we had formed, my husband, R——, M——, and I

Which was the way insecure schoolchildren stood in schoolyards

Not taking any social chances, finishing my Swedish fish, readying to leave

So I could return to my house alone,
to drink alone,
to smoke alone   to be

Alone
    alone
        alone   alone!

I have not been to a party with university faculty since

To be fair, I haven't been invited.

I Have Age Spots Bigger Than Your Balls, Dude

My daughter was home from college for the weekend
We went to see a movie about a missing woman
I had read the book before we went to see the movie
My daughter had started the book but only read it halfway

In the movie a man uses a woman's habit of inebriation to
Convince her she's done terrible things

After the movie we talked about what the man had done

"They call that 'gas-lighting,'" I said.

"Yeah, I mean, I've heard of gas-lighting," she said. "I just didn't know what it was."

My daughter was twenty years old and had just broken up with her boyfriend of five years.

I said, "I've been in two relationships in which, looking back, I see that I felt I needed constantly to prove I was a good person. Or to show I was not a bad person. My morals and values were under constant scrutiny in a way I don't think is healthy."

I laughed. I said, "Thank god I no longer have an interest in representing myself one way or the other."

I was trying to convey to my daughter how getting sucked into viewing yourself as capable of being a good or bad person, takes away your power.

It was part of what I didn't like about *Lemonade*.

"It's human nature to attempt to control another person," I said. "Of course it's harder to recognize our own attempts at control."

"The other day, in fact," I said. "I tried to control your stepfather's drinking due to my own fears of becoming an alcoholic and my childhood feelings of not having any control over the drinking habits of the adults who surrounded and terrified me."

(My daughter was saying things too but I am not quoting my daughter here in order to protect her privacy.)

Once a man had said to me, "I wish you wouldn't view this in terms of power," which was how I knew he viewed our relationship in those terms. It had never occurred to me to view what was happening between us in that way.

That man would have made a good character in a literary thriller in which the word "girl" is in the title.

Then again, I probably would, also.

The Language of Christ

It was two weeks before the election and I was at my hairdresser's in Detroit

My hairdresser was Chaldean and most of her employees were Chaldean and most of her clients also

"We speak the same language as Jesus," she'd told me once

I'd asked a lot of questions over the years

About her culture and religion

"We're from Iraq but we're not Arab. We're Catholics."

"We should write a book together, for Oprah's book club," she'd said

"It'll be about a young divorced Chaldean woman who opens her own hair salon in Detroit and falls in love with a Chaldean man who falls in love with her but won't marry her because his mother doesn't approve of her being divorced," she said

"It'll be a true story," she said

"Okay," I said

"That would probably be a big hit," I said

"But you can't use my real name," she said. "I'll be ostracized from my community," she said

When I'd first met her, working for someone else's salon in a different suburb of Detroit, I'd thought she was Hispanic

She was short and petite and curvy with thick brunette hair

She looked like Eva Longoria

I had a little crush

That was fifteen years ago

My hairdresser had owned two salons since then

"61% of Chaldeans own at least one business," she said

Her husband owned more than one

"party stores" they call them in Detroit

My hairdresser was someone I could talk to in a way I couldn't talk to anyone else; like a priest or therapist

She was very non-judgmental

I'd overheard her reprimanding a young employee recently for making a judgmental comment about Caitlyn Jenner

"You need to be more open minded," she'd told the young woman. "You don't know the opinions and lifestyles of our clients."

It was good practical business advice but it was also genuinely who she was

I'd told her recently about my husband and I having different residences and she'd asked me a bunch of questions about it

"You live such an interesting life," she'd said "Maybe M—— and I should have different houses someday. I think I'd like that"

My hairdresser's parents had emigrated from Iraq with her when she was three or four

"Both of my grandmothers were thirteen when they got married"

She didn't have any baby pictures of herself because they hadn't been able to bring anything to the United States with them when they left Iraq

She didn't have any photos of herself to compare with her own three year old daughter now

On the drive over I'd been thinking about how I never heard anyone from her community profiled on NPR

I'd never heard the word Chaldean until I met my hairdresser

"Do you know who you're going to vote for?" I said

She was blow drying my hair

"What?" she said

She turned the blow dryer away from us

"Who are you voting for?" I repeated

"Trump!" she said

"Do you think most of your community is voting Trump?" I said

"We're all voting Trump!" she said. "We're going to get Trump the vote in Detroit!"

"Who are you voting for?" she said

She'd leaned down toward my ear to ask me, in case I was shy to answer

"Hillary," I said.

"I figured," she said

"Ann Arbor," she said

We were both smiling

I'd assumed she was voting Trump

She'd told me she'd voted for Bush years back

She'd told me her community voted mostly Republican

"What's your main reason for voting Trump?" I said

"The economy!" she said

"Taxes!" she said

"I'm a small business owner and do you know what percentage the money I make goes to taxes and health insurance?"

"Also I want to feel safe. Where I come from, we feared our president. I don't want to fear our president but I want to feel like he's standing up for us and protecting us. I don't feel that way when Obama speaks. He never seems angry."

"Look," she said. "This is the greatest country in the world. Every day I wake up here is a gift. Where else could I go as a small child, could my parents take me, and I grow up to own my own business? This country has opportunities for everyone. Look at N.W.A. . . ."

"The rap group?" I said. I didn't think she meant the rap group.

"Yeah," she said. "Did you see that movie? Look at Dr. Dre. He's a multi-millionaire. Maybe a billionaire. Where else could a black man be a millionaire or billionaire?"

I didn't know. I'd never thought about it. I wiped my eyes. I was getting strangely emotional. The months leading up to the election had been so negative. Everyone was so negative and hateful. Everyone was so angry.

"Look, I don't agree with everything Trump is talking about," she said

"He says a lot of crazy things," she said

"It's the campaign trail," she said

"I wondered if most of your community—being Catholic- was voting Trump because of the abortion issue," I said

She leaned down again

"I think that should be up to the woman," she said

"Personally, I think every woman or girl should decide that for herself," she said

"But you can only vote for one candidate," she said

I nodded

You could only vote for one candidate

You couldn't vote per issue

You couldn't make a moral judgment about a person based on who they voted for

"The number one reason I'm voting for Trump is economics," she said. "That's it. Lower taxes. Lower health care costs."

She was done drying my hair

She was staring at me in the mirror

"The only other place I would ever live is Greece," she said

"Greece?" I said

"I'm teasing, she's from Greece," she said, nodding at the woman in the chair beside me

"No, no," the woman said. "Greece is beautiful but you don't want to live there."

"Were you born there?" my hairdresser asked. "I forget."

"No, no," the woman said. "I was born here. My parents came over before I was born."

"You should ask *her* about politics," my hairdresser said. "She's really into it," she said

"I'm more of a libertarian," the woman said. "You should watch Fox news," the woman said

I laughed.

"She's from *Ann Arbor*," my hairdresser said

"Oh, Ann Arbor," the woman said.

"I'm voting for Trump because I don't want socialized medicine. I don't want to live in a socialist society," the woman said

"Uh huh," I said.

"But I definitely think it's up to the woman," the woman said

"Or girl," my hairdresser said

"Right," I said. "I agree," I said

I was standing now, hovering between chair and door

"Watch Fox News," the woman said

"I gotta go," I said

"Love you," my hairdresser said

"Love you, too," I said

I could have stayed and done a whole journalistic piece on the women in that salon

Or I could have stayed and done research for the novel my hairdresser was always talking about us writing

Instead I wrote this one lousy poem

I don't know; I think it's pretty good

Buckeye State

It was my childhood friend's birthday

I drove to Ohio to see her

She was already drinking with a friend when I got there

It was three o'clock

"Let's go to Happy Hour!" my childhood friend said

I drove my friend and her friend and my friend's husband to Happy Hour

I only drank alone

I made a good Designated Driver

It was an Irish bar

I order a bag of potato chips and a club soda

My friend ordered a gin and tonic

Her husband and friend ordered beers

By eight o'clock my friend and her husband and her friend were soused

We'd gone to dinner and had more drinks

"I don't feel well," my friend said

"I'm trying not to throw up," she said

my friend's daughter was fourteen

she had a brother who was twelve

I went down into the basement with my friend's daughter and son after my friend and her
husband went to bed

My friend's son was playing video games

My friend's daughter showed me various containers of slime she had made

I opened the containers, held my nose to them

They smelled good, like detergent, like cleaning products

"Do you want to make some?" my friend's daughter said

"Okay," I said

"We'll have to go to the store for ingredients," my friend's daughter said

"Okay," I said

It was nine o'clock on a Friday

We went to CVS first but they were out of Elmer's glue

We went to a grocery store; bought glue and Tide and some kind of detergent I'd never
heard of

On the side of the box of detergent I'd never heard of it said, "Not for drug use"

Which was how I knew it was to make drugs

I stood in line with my friend's teenage daughter to buy these cleaning products so we
could make slime

When we got back her brother was still playing video games

We set up all our ingredients on a craft table in the basement

My friend's daughter showed me the order in which to mix the cleaning products

She narrated our entire process

I was starting to feel lightheaded

Like we needed to open a window, but we were in the basement

We were laughing a lot, my friend's daughter and I

"Let's make another batch!" my friend's daughter said

"I'm going to add glitter to mine this time!" she said

I added glitter to mine, too

"I'm going to combine two of mine and make a third," my friend's daughter said

So I combined two of my colors of slime and made a third

"I'm starting to feel like I need a break," I finally said

What I meant was I was beginning to feel really high

I had my three containers of slime to take home with me

My friend's son came into the craft room

I guess he was done playing video games

"Let's play Jenga!" he said

His voice cracked when he said "Jenga"

"In the dark!" he said

His voice cracked when he said "in"

I hated playing Jenga with adults at adult parties but I didn't mind it so much playing it with my friend's kids

It was the most fun I'd had on a Friday in while

I lay on the couch in the dark opening my containers of slime, holding them under my nose

I couldn't inhale deeply enough

I have no memory of falling asleep

Buckeye State II

The next morning I went with my childhood friend and her daughter to a café for coffee

My friend's daughter told my friend how we'd gone to the CVS and then the grocery store, how we'd made three batches of slime and then played Jenga in the dark

"You two would make perfect roommates," my childhood friend said

It was the nicest thing she'd ever told me

I got up to buy a banana

I stood in line next to a group of middle aged white women

The middle aged white women were talking about the election

"I just want to know," one of the women said. "Whether I can not vote for president and still vote the rest of the ballot"

"Sure, you can," one of the other white women said

"That's what I'm planning to do, too," the third said

"I just don't want to vote for either of them," the first woman said

It was the second time in a week I'd heard a (white) woman in a café ask that question, make that statement

Maybe I should have said something

I got my banana and went back to my seat with my friend

The night before we'd been standing in her daughter's bedroom

"*Jennifer*," she'd said "Why'd you draw that Hillary sign on your window? What if your grandma sees it?"

Earlier in the evening my childhood friend had told me about Jennifer being in a feminist play at her high school

"It's set in the 1800s and is about a woman whose husband has her committed even though she's not crazy," my childhood friend said "It's really powerful," she said

"I wish I could see it," I said

"Jennifer and her girlfriends are really into the LGBTQ and feminist movements," she said

Earlier she'd told me Jennifer had a girlfriend, had taken her girlfriend to homecoming

"I don't really like Hillary, either," my childhood friend had said, after asking Jennifer why she'd drawn Hillary's name on her window

I didn't say anything

I felt differently but she hadn't asked me how I felt

"I'll probably vote for her, but I don't really like her," my friend said

I wanted to say something positive about Hillary and feminism because Jennifer was still in the room but I didn't know what to say or how to say it

My friend went to get a drink of water and I sat on Jennifer's bed opening containers of slime and asking her about the books on her bookshelf, about the quotes on her wall

One of the quotes said, "Pretty on the outside, but DYING within. That's me."

Her mother came back into the room and said, "What does that even mean?"

I wanted to say something positive about Hillary

"You better wash that off your window," my childhood friend said

Censorship Is Obscene

I was a student at the University of Cincinnati when the Robert Mapplethorpe exhibit at the Contemporary Art Museum was shut down

Or I was living in Cincinnati and telling my family I was a student at the time

I can't remember which

I was a student for a year and then I was put on academic probation and then I wasn't a student anymore

But I still collected checks from my grandmother as though I were

My friends and my boyfriend were students of the art college at UC

(I had briefly been an English major)

The contemporary art museum in Cincinnati was on trial

We marched in black t-shirts that said, "Censorship Is Obscene"

Which seems in direct contrast to how young people view art and literature and film today

Our opposition—old white Republican men—talked about the safety of the children and young adults viewing such "pornographic" material

We marched in support of it, of our choice to view or not view photographs of penises and assholes, unclothed males, black and white, whips and bondage

Tipper Gore was fighting to get labels on CDs and album covers, because of "controversial" musical groups like 2 Live Crew and Judas Priest

She was fighting to protect the minds and ears of our generation, to keep us "safe"

We hated Tipper Gore

We were young *adults*

We didn't need or want to feel "safe"

We wanted to experience the world, *all of it*

"Die for your art" was another slogan we wore on t-shirts and pins

Andy Warhol and Keith Haring and Robert Mapplethorpe and Basquiat were *our artists*

Each was or would be dead soon

I don't know what artists young people look up to today

I don't know if anyone is dying for her art

Email and tell me: ee@hobartpulp.com

No Shit, Sherlock

I was skimming a biography of Sir Arthur Conan Doyle that had belonged to my
    grandfather

I stumbled onto a passage that said Arthur Doyle's mother had been seventeen, his father
    twenty-two, when they married

I set the book upside down on my lap in order to more freely scream

I said, "AAAAARRRGGGGGH!

[there was no one but me, two dogs, a cat and a lizard, in my house]

I said, "Take a step back from the fucking forest people!"

[I was, as usual, talking to myself]

It had been two years and I still could not believe anyone would label someone a 'rapist'
    for having sex with a seventeen year old when he was twenty-two

I could not believe that people who considered themselves writers and artists and
    intellectuals were suddenly looking to the LAW to decide their ethics and morality

I wanted to ask IF ROE V WADE IS OVERTURNED AND ABORTION IS OUTLAWED WILL
    YOU SUDDENLY BELIEVE ABORTION TO BE IMMORAL OR UNETHICAL

WILL YOU SUDDNLY REFER TO ANYONE WHO HAS AN ABORTION AS A
    "MURDERER"?!

I sent my husband a text about Sir Arthur Conan Doyle's parents' ages at the time of their
    marriage

I said, "my head just wants to explode at the idea of ppl labeling —— a rapist"

My husband texted back, "Haha"

"It's not funny!" I said. "They are trying to ruin his career, his livelihood!"

"I didn't mean haha funny," my husband said. "Just re your head exploding. And also ridiculouness of it. I don't really know how to respond to ppl being crazy other than to go 'haha.'"

"oh," I said

"haha," I said

Difficult Women

I was watching old reruns of *Roseanne*

Wondering where she'd gone

I'd listened to her interview on Marc Maron

Talking about her teen years locked up in a mental ward

Her runaway years

Her years as a young mom before she got called over by Carson

She was a feminist icon

I wanted to tweet at her "MOM" but I didn't have a Twitter

She only had 300 k followers

A small number for someone who tweeted a lot

She supported Trump

All her recent tweets were about him

Or about how she hated Hillary

—a longstanding feud resulting from her talk show cancellation the day after she'd interviewed one of Bill's accusers—

I thought this was a feminist option - despising another woman

I was reading *The Godfather*

I identified equally with Michael Corleone

" . . . don't let anybody kid you. It's all personal, every bit of business. Every piece of shit every man has to eat every day of his life is personal. They call it business. OK. But it's personal as hell."

Michael gave that speech before he shot the man who tried to kill his father

I started reading Roseanne's Twitter for the same reason I read Megan Boyle's

Because they were at least being honest (honest to themselves, I mean)

(and because I couldn't shoot anyone)

I clicked an audio link on Roseanne's Twitter, listened to Roseanne talk about brainwashing and code words

Roseanne said people used labels like "racist" and "sexist" and "homophobic" to discourage dissenting voices, to end discussions, to silence opposition

I didn't agree with a lot of what Roseanne said but I thought about the code words and the overuse of such labels and the way in which they were used, as fear tactics, to silence

I thought about how the morning my essay was published, the initial responses were complex, the overriding decision regarding it not yet fixed or decided

I remembered how Kate Zambreno had tweeted a link to my essay and said I had some interesting thoughts

An hour later, she had removed the tweet

I remembered Sheila Heti initially tweeting she wasn't going to be calling anyone a rapist and how later she not only deleted that tweet, but deleted her entire Twitter

I remembered emailing a young woman that weekend to say I understood if she didn't want to read with me the following month

The essay opposing me, labeling me, had not yet gone up

The young woman had replied on Sunday that while she didn't agree with much of what I said in my essay, she *of course* was open to discussing it, she was, *of course*, still wanting to read with me

But the Monday the opposing essay was published, the same young woman emailed me again to say she had reread my essay, to say I had said "a lot of fucked up things," to say she no longer wanted to read with me

The brainwashing had begun, discussions halted

By code words ("rape apologist") and by fear of association with them, of being labeled the same

People who had texted or emailed me support or admiration over the weekend, went suddenly quiet; deleted links to my essay from their social media

Being a "difficult woman" could be a career wrecker

Being associated with one, the same

Roseanne only has 300k followers

I don't think she's deleting any tweets

A BIGOT IS A BIGOT IS A BIGOT

I was looking at Twitter

A friend had retweeted another friend who had made the proclamation that "all Trump supporters are racist and homophobic and xenophobes"

I wasn't sure the people making such proclamations (or retweeting them) understood the word "bigotry"

I wasn't sure why it wasn't offensive for a liberal male talk show host to ask a conservative female one why she was so angry

I couldn't imagine anyone asking Roxane was she was so angry and getting away with it (with not being called condescending and misogynistic, I mean)

The Russians Love Their Children Too

In the mid '80s we were afraid of the Russians -

that they were going to bomb us or 'nuke' us or something

I don't know/It's hard to remember

Tears for Fears was really popular that year

Also that year that female teacher burned up in the spaceship

We all watched it on TV

I was living with my mother and her boyfriend in an apartment in Mesa, Arizona

The year before I had gone to a boarding school in central Florida

The next year we would move back to Ohio

It was exactly how every teenager foresees her teen years unfolding: in three different states!

My school in Mesa, Arizona was more diverse than the one I had gone to in Ohio

There were black people and Hispanic people and guys who surfed

In my Arizona History class there was a girl with thick magenta bangs cut straight across her eyebrows

She wore combat boots and black tights and a jean jacket that said, THE RUSSIANS LOVE THEIR CHILDREN TOO across the back of it

"Russians (Love Their Children Too)" was a popular song by Sting in 1985 or '86

I keep thinking about that jacket (but not the song) now that our country is so divided

I think it would be a good reminder

Not about the Russians, but, you know

"If You Love Somebody Set Them Free" was a much more popular Sting song that year)

FEAR & LOATHING & 1%-ers

I was in another bar, listening to anther group of 1%-ers talk about their fears of a Trump presidency

(They were 1%-ers as far as their levels of education in this country, I mean)

Everyone was drinking craft beers and vodka tonics and talking about how they couldn't stand Hillary and talking about how much of their time was taken up with parenting

Most of the writers I knew had two degrees, a good handful of them three

I understood they needed the degrees in order to make a living and that I had inherited money so I didn't

Later they would be angry with people on the right for their alleged racism and I would be angry with the people on the left for their denied sexism

(I'd heard plenty of people say "I'm not going to vote for someone just because she's a woman" but I hadn't heard anyone say eight years earlier, "I'm not going to vote for someone just because he's black.")

It all came out even in the end

A man with a beard compared Trump to Hitler in the same way conservatives had compared Obama to Hitler, drawing a tiny moustache over a poster of the president early in his first term

Another man with a beard used the term "fascists" and a woman with a lot of arm tattoos used the term "Nazis" which seemed slightly to contradict one another or to be not quite the correct terminology and again seemed to mimic words used by the right to criticize Obama but what did I know

I wasn't very political

And anyway I was already fearful

I'd been fearful for a while now

The bearded men and that tattooed woman had never had a reading cancelled because someone didn't feel safe with them in a bookstore

The bearded men and tattooed woman had gotten nice reviews for their books in *The New York Times* and small but nonetheless noteworthy mentions in the 'Fan Fare' section of *Vanity Fair*, the editor of which shared an agent with at least one of them

The tattooed woman was talking about abortion rights and how the government needed to keep its hands off her body but she didn't seem to feel the same when it came to regulating age of consent or age of nicotine sales or age of alcohol sales

I didn't want any of the above dictated by the government

Which, I guess, in my mind then, made the tattooed woman a fascist

The bearded men had not committed any crimes in their teen years that had placed them on A LIST well into their thirties, and caused them considerable hardship as far as finding employment and housing and as far as not being feared and discriminated against decades after their crimes and incarcerations, in a manner that was unjust and inhumane, as a friend of mine had

(at least not any crimes for which they were caught and legally punished)

I viewed the sex offenders' list as cruel and unusual punishment (fascism? Nazism?)

So far none of the bearded men or the tattooed woman had lost their jobs at the university for making an inappropriate statement or for teaching an inappropriate text

So far none of them had asked a question that had gone against the group think ideology and caused them to be blacklisted or censored or isolated from the group

And most likely they would be careful not to ask such questions or to make such statements

And so they would be *safe*

In their employment and in their community

Later I emailed my stepfather

I said, "The people in my community say that anyone who votes for Trump is sexist and racist and homophobic."

"Maybe you need new friends," my stepfather said

"That is the most shallow thinking," he said

I said, "They say people on the right are fascists and Nazis."

"Think about if you reversed that statement," he said

I had reversed it, earlier in the poem, but he didn't know that (yet)

Ms. Magazine

for HRC

I gave this section of poems to two friends to read

They both said the same thing

I was too angry

I didn't have a right to be so angry

Sure, one of my friends said, People had hurt me, had judged me unfairly, but that didn't give me the right

I respectfully disagreed

I thought it did (give me the right)

I thought it was a problem of a woman being angry

Or maybe I was angry about the wrong things, at the wrong people

Maybe my friends thought I was angry with them

And maybe I (subconsciously) was

My daughter said she was offended every time I said, "all young people" in my poems

I said, "I don't think I ever say 'all'"

"You know what I mean," my daughter said

It was true, I did (know)

"I guess I probably sound old and bitter," I said

"Yeah," my daughter said. "You sound a little bitter."

There was another email from my friend

You aren't being self-critical enough, she said

I saw her point—

For once I wasn't making myself the most hated person in the poem

For once I wasn't self-loathing (enough)

I had moved on to loathing everyone else

As a coping mechanism, I mean

As a way to feel something different, a new emotion

The old Eugene O'Neill quote again (only so much blame you can take before turning it
back on someone else . . .)

Last week I listened to an interview with the man who wrote *Taxi Driver*

The man who wrote *Taxi Driver* said it was a very "adolescent" film

He was twenty-six when he wrote it, he said; depressed, angry

I am forty-seven, depressed, angry

Some of these poems are very *adolescent*

I'll be the second (or third or fourth) to admit that

But to remove them would be to remove a part of me

And I want you to see *all my parts!*

I was reading *The Godfather* also this week (oh, did I already say this?)

The great thing about a horse head in someone's bed is how *not* passive aggressive it can
seem while being *totally* passive aggressive

Helter Swelter

I was driving and it was summer and my daughter was in the car and my daughter was
   texting

I said, "we should do away w age, as a system. Then we wouldn't have to deal with these
   dumb laws"

My daughter was eighteen, nineteen, I forget which
I'd been telling her about how our city was going to be the first in the state to raise the
   tobacco sale age to twenty-one

"yup," my daughter said

"are you listening?" I said.

"what did you say?" my daughter said.

"I said we should do away with age altogether, which is just another man made system . . . "

"Like the calendar?"

"yeah, all of it . . .

"wtf. you sound like a communist"

"I knew you weren't listening, " I said.

Feminism

for CVW
for HRC

We were on our way to a Hillary rally in Detroit

My friend and my friend's two year old daughter and I

My friend had made us flower crowns, "like the suffragettes," she said—which made me think of Motown, which was a few streets over

My friend's daughter pulled hers off almost immediately
"Hurts! Hurts!" she said

We kept walking and walking and walking, the line went four or five blocks

There were secret service men and women on the tops of every nearby building

A young man in line behind us was a vocal Trump supporter

He seemed to want our attention

My knee jerk response was to ignore him
It was my go-to way of handling most situations involving other humans

But my friend engaged with him, spoke to him in her professorial voice, with respect or whatever

I'm sure it made him feel 'heard' or listened to or something
Maybe she hoped it would make him hate women less—
Or make him respect us more or, you know . . .

I was chasing her toddler down an alleyway
Her daughter was fast for a two year old
My daughter was in college
I didn't have any reason to run anymore

Four months earlier I'd written an email with the subject line "feminism" and sent it to this woman and two others

I'd found myself in a weakened state, sobbing in the shower, before writing the email

Later I showed my daughter the email I'd written and the responses

(I'd been sitting with a towel wrapped around my waist on a barstool in our kitchen, hair dripping down my back onto the floor, still crying, when I'd written it)

I could tell it bothered my daughter, seeing me in this vulnerable state in which I'd put myself in an attempt at getting these three women to talk to me

I could tell she was embarrassed (for me)

One of the women was the creator and star of a TV show my daughter and I had watched together the previous four years

The woman's reply was brief but kind, considering we had never met or emailed before, considering I'd gotten her email address from an email forwarded from a mutual friend, considering how "insane" I sounded in my email, according to my daughter

Another woman had been an early champion of my writing and had become famous for hers, which was political and taken seriously and read by people like my best friend from grade school and my mother

Her reply was long and I had avoided reading it, perhaps fearing her strength and decisiveness, but my daughter read it and said, "she makes good points," which didn't make me want to read it either

I was a coward like that
I wanted to be heard but I didn't want to listen
I was terrified of rejection,
Of being ostracized, even though that was what had prompted my email in the first place

There wasn't an email reply from my friend because my friend had immediately called me when she received my email

Initially, when I'd seen her call come through, I'd panicked; let it go to voicemail

We'd never spoken on the phone
She'd only recently moved to my city; we'd been long distance acquaintances more than friends prior to that

She sent a quick follow up text, "I don't get it. Do you want to talk or not?"

I liked the judgment and challenge of that text, she seemed to be calling me on my shit

(I instantly liked anyone who called me on my shit)

I was still crying when I dialed her number

I was really self-indulging in the moment

It'd been two years of telling myself I didn't care and now I cared and I wanted someone to listen

I had chosen the three women to whom I had sent the email because each of them was known for her feminism and I believed myself to be a feminist and I wanted to engage in conversations with feminists

I had said something in the email about feeling blacklisted and about wanting to talk—publicly or privately—about topics I had discussed in the essay that had gotten me blacklisted which I considered women's issues or feminist issues or both

I complained in the email that my husband had not been blacklisted, even though he had read the essay before I published it and cried while reading it and even though it had been published on the website he had founded and still edited

I complained that the female authors I published were championed for their books but that I was not championed for publishing them in the way I thought a female publisher of female authors would be championed if the female publisher weren't blacklisted

I was really self-indulging!

My friend asked me what had prompted me to write the email and I told her about the continued blacklisting and ostracizing and gas-lighting which had gone on now for two years

"The gas-lighting is the worst," I said. "Even my husband and friends of mine will make me feel like I'm being paranoid or jumping to conclusions, because most people don't say outright, 'we're not publishing you or booking you or replying to your email because of your essay.' So I'm constantly wondering if things are coincidental or malicious. If I've just suddenly become a shittier writer who can't write anything worth publishing, or if people genuinely hate me."

"Yeah," my friend said in a soft soothing voice. I could imagine her working a suicide hotline with that voice. "That must be really hard. I'll admit, it's hard to be associated with you. And with that anthology, I didn't pull out for a couple reasons, one being that I was up for a job and I didn't want to blow it."

"Thank you for telling me that," I said.

I don't remember the rest of the conversation

We were on the phone thirty minutes, an hour

There were elements of our childhoods and experiences with our mother that had brought us together almost ten years earlier

We had always meant, I think, to become good friends

When she asked me months after that phone conversation to go with her to the Hillary rally I was excited by the invitation

Not only for the opportunity to see our first female presidential candidate

But also for the opportunity to share the moment with her and her daughter

I had admittedly been drawn to and skeptical of her in the weeks between that call and the day of the rally

I felt hesitant to fully trust her

I thought at any moment it might again become too problematic, being associated with me

I kept waiting for the invitations to dry up
For her to stop returning my texts

I told myself we weren't *really* friends

We were each just drawn to the entertainment of interacting with one another

We were each of us seeing how far it could go

And then suddenly it began to feel like a bad romantic comedy storyline:

"And then while *pretending* to fall in love, they fall in love"

Except in my case, instead of continuing to feign friendship, it began to feel slowly—and, to me—like actual friendship

Inside the building in Detroit, my friend sat on the cement floor with her toddler and I squatted on the base of a pole next to them, a giant American flag hung at our backs A local pastor took the stage, then Hillary

We had waited in line for two hours

My friend's daughter had eaten blueberries and goldfish crackers and a granola bar and fruit gummies

We had each held our place in line while the other chased after the toddler

My daughter had texted me, "I wish I was there with you but I'm glad you're there!"

In front of us at the back of the crowd, a man in his fifties stood beside his father in a wheelchair in his eighties

I watched them exchange regular glances, clapping and cheering and nodding their heads in unison, one time raising a fist

I missed my grandfather

I was warmed by the men's shared participation in this historical event

I was still shy around my friend when it came to true moments of intimacy

I was aware of the times we each clapped simultaneously, but I did not turn to her as the man turned to his father; I did not share that visual unity, that nodding of heads

On the drive home my friend seemed disappointed

Earlier in the summer my friend had said something like, "You set up situations for closeness and then back out of them"

I was trying to be a strong woman, unaffected

Part of the freeway was shut down so that Hillary could get to the airport

I still didn't trust that inner voice that kept insisting we were friends

It took us an hour and a half to get home, twice as long as the drive to get there

I said, "Do you have any more of those goldfish [her daughter] was eating?"

"Sure," she said. "They're down in that blue bag. Good idea. I'm hungry, too."

I opened the bag between my knees and we took turns reaching our hands into the bag.

Chinese Restaurant II — Blonde on Blonde

What about Dylan?

Nu uh

David Foster Wallace?

Nope

Jay Z?

Uh uh

Tarantino?

Nada

Seinfeld?

Noooo

Louis CK?

I laughed

We were talking about *Lemonade*

We were talking about the Nobel Prize

We were talking about problematic men

"Everyone's a victim or a villain now," I said.

"Not even a victim and a *hero*," my friend said. (Or maybe my husband said that, later, when I was telling him the story.)

"I'm not one to listen to gossip," my friend said. "But one of our mutual friends told me that a man I'm supposed to read with this weekend, a man up for some book award or something, was allegedly abusive to his ex girlfriend, who is a friend of our mutual friend."

"Hmmm," I said.

"I don't know him," I said.

Later my husband said, "Pretty much everyone who's gone through a breakup could say the other person was emotionally abusive on some level, though."

"Right," I said, wondering in what ways my husband thought me emotionally abusive.

"If you stay together any length of time," I said

"It's going to get ugly at some point," my husband said

I've known my husband fourteen years—

I didn't have enough hands to count how many times.

Ask the Dust

I'd been watching an old '70s sitcom on my breaks from writing poems

The sitcom was about a single mother and her son living in Arizona

This morning when I brushed my teeth there was blood in the sink

In one episode the single mother is mistakenly arrested for prostitution

In another she finds a photograph of a naked woman in her twelve year old son's wallet

I remembered Fante and Bukowski writing about bleeding while brushing their teeth

I thought, "aha! I'm finally 'a writer'!"

Don't Look Back/Fat Steve Buscemi

I was having drinks with a man I had met twenty years ago and hadn't seen since
People used to tell the man he resembled the actor Steve Buscemi
Now he looked like a fat Steve Buscemi

He said, "Yeah, but Dylan never had a number one hit."

The day before they had announced Bob Dylan being awarded the Nobel Prize (in
   Literature)

"The Rolling Stones had a number one hit," Fat Steve Buscemi said

"Yeah," I said. "But did The Rolling Stones ever get booed?"

"What?" said Fat Steve Buscemi.

"Nothing," I said. "I was thinking of something else," I said.

Fat Steve Buscemi had gone to acting school or taken acting lessons years earlier when he
   was thin and lived for a brief time in L.A.

I liked Fat Steve Buscemi but he didn't know shit about Bob Dylan.

I paid for our drinks and we left the bar.

They were playing an old Edie Brickell song as we left.
I walked out of the bar thinking of how Paul Simon had married Edie Brickell and how we
   hadn't heard from her since.

Bob Dylan left Joan Baez and Joan Baez continued to make music, kept making records

What I am is what I am are you what you are or what?

No one under the age of 35 will get the above reference because of Paul Simon but also
   because of Edie Brickell

Fat Steve Buscemi didn't know shit.

Only a Pawn in Their Game (for Bob)

I.

I was watching a documentary about Bob Dylan (*No Direction Home*)
This was before they announced he'd won the Nobel Prize (in literature)
The night before the announcement, to be specific
I'd been on a Dylan kick all autumn
I don't remember what got me started

Dylan was talking about being an outsider
In the documentary, I mean
Reflecting on his time in New York City in the early '60s

He said, "They were trying to make me an insider to some kind of trip they were on. I
    don't think so."

It was the "I don't think so" that got me.

I felt similarly about the feminist movement
I felt similarly about all movements, to be fair

A woman on the radio proclaiming to be a feminist last week had said, "It's great when we
    have one voice."

I shook my head at the radio.

I wanted whatever men had and I had never known men to have one voice.

Days later, someone from The Nobel committee was quoted as saying Dylan was arrogant
    because he hadn't yet acknowledged The Nobel committee.

The easiest thing in the world would have been for me to write that *Jezebel* essay the way
    they wanted me to write it.

II.

I was reading a book about Dylan and Joan Baez (*Positively 4th Street*)
It was about Joan Baez's sister Mimi and Mimi's husband too
Mimi's husband was a writer who'd gone to school with Pynchon
He'd died on the release day of his first novel
(Mimi's husband, I mean)

In the book, the book's author (David Hajdu) discusses one of Bob's songs,
"Only a Pawn in Their Game"
It was about the death of Medgar Evers, he said
But it was also about the "web of culpability in a world fraught with racial conflict and
    poverty"
[Hajudu] said Dylan "continued to exonerate a southern politician preaching racial
    superiority"
And "devoted three out of his five verses to a sympathetic treatment of poor whites in a
    song titularly about the death of a Negro martyr"
[Hajudu] said, "There are no easy answers in 'Only a Pawn in Their Game'"
Instead, [Hajudu] said the song, "raises thorny questions: Where does social responsibility
    begin and end? Can exploitation be excused? When does the one in power become a
    pawn?"

It sounded like Dylan was a white supremacist apologist
(in today's language, I mean)
it sounded like Dylan had empathy for or at least a want to understand
a cold blooded murderer
It sounded like Dylan was asking questions when what the country wanted or (thought it)
    needed was one voice in answer

I can already feel my husband rolling his eyes at this poem.

Well-Adjusted Women

I was talking with my friend C. on the phone
I was telling her I'd been going to bed before midnight and not drinking
She was telling me about a memoir she'd just read about a woman with a drinking
    problem

"Every memoir," I said

I wanted to read it like everyone else, though
I already had a sample downloaded on my Kindle

"What if one of us wrote a memoir about how 'normal' and 'well-adjusted' we are now,"
    I said

"Haha," C. said.

"'And then I got another good night's sleep!'" I said.

"'And then I woke up refreshed and ready for the day!'" C. said

"'I didn't stalk any exes online or drink a bottle of wine or smoke cigarettes!'" I said

"Snoozefest," C. said

"Unmarketable," I said

Well-Adjusted Women II

I was thumbing through a magazine at one in the morning in lieu of drinking or sleeping
  or using the internet (my laptop was in a closet of my neighbor's house)

I paused on a page in which an older Italian man in the fashion industry was asked a series
  of questions like what was his favorite restaurant and what was his favorite stationary

I studied the man's answers
The man answered that he liked white velvet pants and sleeping nude

The man was asked what websites he reads on a daily basis

The man said, "I don't like to surf. I worry that it'll take away time from my spirit"

I thought about his answer for a while

I figured something had been lost in translation

American people tended not to speak of their spirits

I considered getting rid of my laptop permanently rather then temporarily leaving it at
  my neighbor's house (I don't own a smart phone)

Like an old white male privileged writer

Or the editor of The Pushcart Prize

I imagined conducting all business via snail mail and a landline telephone

I imagined purchasing a pair of white velvet pants, sleeping nude

But it was so cold in Michigan

And I was afraid of becoming a well-adjusted woman,

How I would ever get published if that happened

Well-Adjusted Women III

I was having dinner with C.
I'd just picked her up from the airport
The next day we were going to Vegas; I couldn't fly alone

"I was in New York City all last week," C. said

"You wouldn't believe this meeting I had," C. said

"It was like an episode of *Girls*," she said

C. was having the sort of meetings I would be having if I had written a different sort of essay for *Jezebel* instead of the essay I wrote for *Hobart* two years ago

C. was trying to explain the nature of the company, the various wings: literary, videography, podcasts

"I don't get it," I said

"Yeah, no one does," she said

"Even the guy I took the meeting with, the cofounder of the company. He just kept rubbing his face in his hands. I would show you but it would irritate my acne," she said

"He told me the name of a writer whose book they're publishing—their first one. He told me she'd been raped four times and is from a middle eastern country. 'That's the sort of writer we're looking for,' he said. 'The sort of books we are interested in publishing. We've exhausted the New York writers.'"

"He wants to pay me to recruit writers for him," she said. "He asked me if seven thousand was enough."

"Dollars?" I said

"Yeah," she said "They have all this money they don't know what to do with," she said

"I've had two abortions, sign me up," I said

"Abortions probably aren't interesting anymore," I said

"Abortions are out," C. said

"Abortion culture is so '90s," I said

"It'll come back around," I said

"If Trump gets elected," C. said

"Then I'll get paid," I said

"Don't ever repeat this conversation," C. said

Well-Adjusted Women IV

My friend said, "Did I ever tell you about the press release they sent out with my first book?"

"No," I said

My friend and I were at a vegan café
I was eating vegan macaroni and cheese

My friend's first book had won several awards

It was a collection of stories; my husband and I had published one of the stories

"I wouldn't have known except a man wrote a review of my book on Goodreads in which he made a comment about my mother having had a number of boyfriends. I made a comment underneath his review, asking him why he said that since there was no reference to that in my book. The man apologized, said he'd thought it was okay to talk about since it'd been mentioned in the press release that came with the galley of the book. I found out later the press release also mentioned my father being in the Manson Family," she said

"I asked the publisher for the press release but they wouldn't let me see it," she said

"They said they would cease using it and I could see the new one but they wouldn't show me the original," she said

"Wow," I said
"I can't believe they would do that," I said

"There's nothing in any of your stories about that," I said

"I know," she said

"Four rapes," I thought. "Manson Family," I thought.

I couldn't think of anything in my background that was so easily marketable.

"Mother married and divorced three times before I was twelve," I thought

I'd used that line a lot in the beginning, I remembered

"Schizophrenic husband," I thought

I'd used that a couple times, too

Later, after lunch, I read an article online about the actress Shelly Duvall

People on social media were angry that Dr. Phil had shamelessly filmed and promoted her erratic behavior, her apparent mental illness

A child of Stanley Kubrick—who had directed Shelly in *The Shining*—called it "disgusting" and "reprehensible"

It's a fine line, I thought, between "bringing awareness" to a topic and capitalizing on someone's tragedy

And the line seemed always to be moving

I could no longer locate the line

Kenny Loggins Letter

I was drinking wine and watching a TV show about a serial killer

The actor who played the serial killer was beautiful in the way a young horse is beautiful

Meaning, you figured while watching the TV show you'd be okay with him killing you

I figured it was the same thing with Leonardo DiCaprio, like, no one was ever going to accuse Leonardo of date rape or sexual assault

He could put his hand under any woman's skirt or dress on any airplane always

It was just a fact

It was two in the morning when I checked my email

It was five days before the election

I was too moody to talk to friends

I had gotten in a fight with my husband the night before

He'd been mid-frying an egg

He had scooped the partially fried egg onto a paper plate, taken it with him to his apartment on the other side of town

I had run a hot bath; read several magazines

There was an email in my inbox from a writer with whom I had a fickle relationship

I had often remarked of the writer, "If she were a man, I'd be madly in love with her"

(She was smart and darkly humorous and tortured and I couldn't get a read on how she felt about me)

Since she wasn't a man (and there didn't seem to be any physical attraction between us), I was constantly torn between phasing her out of my life and making plans to see her three times a week

There was some bad blood between us, but the bad blood was what kept me coming back
I was repelled by simplicity or I was drawn toward the complex

The email was a forward from a literary magazine run by a celebrity

The writer who had forwarded it had written in the space above the email, "I looked through all my contacts and I don't know anyone who would vote for Trump—maybe forward this to someone you know?"

I was already offended

I wasn't sure how she knew who people she knew would vote for

I thought, isn't this part of the problem of the divide in our country? Not knowing anyone with opinions and ideas that don't match your own?

It felt as though she were bragging

About being so isolated in academia

This was the source of my fight with my husband also: the academic bubble

Recently we had walked my in laws through the English building at the university that employs my husband

On every wall was a sign that said, "Racism will not be tolerated"

Nothing was said about sexism (despite a woman running for president and people on both sides very vocally expressing hatred for her) or terrorism (despite there being incidents of terror on college campuses)

Nothing was said about homophobia (and I noticed a grimace on my father-in-law's face as he read the flyer for a lecture about rural gays and lesbians—even though he planned, as usual, to vote Democratic; a lecture my daughter and I made a note to attend)

I had confided in? told? the writer that I knew several people who were probably going to vote for Trump—relatives, friends, some in their early 20s, others who were 60, 70, 90

It seemed like I was supposed to be ashamed to admit this

It seemed like I was supposed to offer an explanation for their voting

That it was my responsibility to humanize 'them' to her

The email from the celebrity-run literary journal contained a series of essays and comics and drawings, all meant to explain things like sexism and date rape and the Muslim culture in America to a ten year old

Or maybe an eight year old

It was hard to tell the age of the child the email was meant for

And at the top of the email it was explained that the celebrity-run journal had realized that they'd been 'preaching to the choir,' that they needed to do more 'outreach,' and so, could you, liberal, *not* racists, *not* homophobic, *not* sexist person reading this, please forward the email to someone you know, you know, like a *friend*, who *is* homophobic and/or racist and/or sexist, thanks!

I was offended

By the self-righteousness of the email written by the celebrity-run journal's editor(s)

And by the "I can't find *anyone* in *my contacts* who would vote for Trump" implied witch hunt of the writer who had forwarded it to me

It was two a.m. and I'd been watching a TV show about a hot serial killer and I was a little drunk on red wine

I wrote back

I said that I'd found the whole email condescending, that I wasn't going to be forwarding it to anyone

I said that if she didn't think 'we' were racist and sexist, she should think again

I said that voting a certain party line did not mean anything re racism or sexism or homophobia

I confided in her people I knew who voted Democratic and had been and maybe still were against gay marriage for religious reasons

I pointed out the hatred of Hillary in our own party

I might have, but didn't, pointed out her stating that she was more often friends with men than women and how I understood what she meant because I had once stated the same (it was easier to be friends with men, they overlooked more, they flattered you, being friends with women was tougher, more challenging, as she and I have proven)

I didn't mention but thought of all the 'liberal' parents I knew who had been relieved when their child hadn't yet turned out to be gay

I thought of a million ways in which I and every single person I knew could be accused of racism

I said I thought we would do better to look inside ourselves and work on improving ourselves before trying to 'educate' those we don't know personally

I was emboldened by the red wine and the late hour

I later wondered if my reply sounded self-righteous or condescending

I later wrote an apology, saying I had taken out my frustrations re the election and everything regarding it on her

But in that moment, at two in the morning, five days before the election, I didn't really give a fuck

Empathy Exams II, AKA Cold-Hearted Cynic Like You

It was Thanksgiving and I was watching *Planes, Trains, and Automobiles* on a folding chair in my basement with my family

I had seen the movie many times

I was reciting every line in my head three seconds before it was spoken

I had forgotten how early on Steve Martin yells at John Candy

I had thought that scene was halfway or three quarters way through the movie

Instead it was the first night they share a motel room

John Candy is quiet for a two full minutes while Steve Martin lists all the things John Candy has done and said that have annoyed him

It's a long list

Finally Steve Martin stops talking

He seems exhausted by his own anger

Finally it's John Candy's turn to talk

John Candy says (paraphrasing), "You can say what you want about me, I'm not going to change, I like me, my customers like me, my family likes me, my wife likes me"

Of course we know his wife is dead (spoiler alert!) but that's beside the point

I thought about myself, about the accusations against me, the labels I'd been given, and I agreed with John Candy

I thought, "Say what you want about me, call me what you want. I like me. I like having empathy—or attempting to have empathy—for everyone (or disdain for everyone, equally)"

I thought, "Cuz I'm the real article—what ya see, is what ya get"

I thought, "I am, whatever you say I am, if I wasn't, then why would I say I am? In the papers, the news, every day I am, I don't know, it's just the way I am"

Because I also identified strongly with an angry blonde male rapper

Bukowski

for Papa Jack

This morning I cried reading a Bukowski poem

It was the one from *Love Is A Dog From Hell* called

'how to be a great writer'

I cried because I missed Bukowski and my grandfather

I missed the kind of man who isn't living for anyone else

I yearned to live as honestly

Before he died (in 1999) my grandfather gave me the *Manual for Writers & Editors*

He'd always wanted to be a writer

Inside he wrote, "Beth – Maybe you will write the book we dreamed about, hope this helps. DO IT!"

But he was born in 1918

To a pair of second generation German immigrants

His mother, Adra, quit school in the ninth grade to work in a maraschino cherry factory

(her hands were red for two years, she later told me)

(she lied about her age to get the job, she said)

His father, "Young," lost an eye (and contracted prostate cancer) in the factory where he worked for thirty years

My grandfather didn't have the luxury of being a writer

So he became an engineer instead

Drank gin and passed out on the toilet

Smoked cigarettes until he was coughing up blood

My grandfather never read Bukowski,

would have thought him too low brow

My grandfather read Wodehouse and (Sherlock) and *The New Yorker* in his later years

Got The Clap in the war

Stopped speaking to friends when his wife left him for another man (a doctor)

Walked right past *her*, my grandmother, without speaking when he ran into her at the
    club twenty years later . . .

The man could hold a grudge!

I missed my grandfather

I felt very protective of him

I cried reading this poem by ole Bukowski:

and remember the old dogs
who fought so well:
Hemingway, Celine, Dostoyevsky, Hamsun.

if you think they didn't go crazy
in tiny rooms
just like you're doing now

without women
without food
without hope

then you're not ready.

drink more beer.
there's time.
and if there's not
that's all right
too.

I cried because there was a vulnerability in Bukowski's writing

A loneliness and beauty that is now forgotten

I felt very protective of ole Bukowski

Let me know when anyone else writes as honestly!

Election

for Andie
and for HRC

My daughter was voting at her university, an hour away

It was her first time voting in a presidential election

She texted me early in the morning, "Wear white for the suffragettes!"

She had classes all day, her job as a lab assistant in the evening

I was a freelance writer

I got to vote at noon

My polling station was her elementary school

It was a five minute walk from our house

The back of the line was in the hall outside her third grade classroom

The woman in front of me in line was on her cell phone

She said, "Did she ever lie under oath?"

I strained to hear more of the conversation

I was curious myself, now that she'd brought it up, even though I didn't give a shit one
way or the other

The woman said, "I don't know. ABC didn't cover it. I don't even think Fox covered it."

It was an interesting distinction, lying under oath versus just plain lying

Twice my daughter had run for class president, in 3rd and 4th grades

I had admired her tenacity, her unwillingness to run for a lesser office after the initial
defeat

In fifth grade she'd been the target of bullying by a male classmate, which led to bullying
by a handful of male classmates

375

On three different occasions I sat in the principal's office, pleading for the school to do
 something

I said, "Every day at recess my eleven year old daughter is being called a 'slut' and a
 'whore,' the boys tell her repeatedly to 'suck my dick', tell her she's fat."

The principal, who was a woman, refused to move the boy into another classroom or to
 punish the boy

She said she had spoken with the boy's parents

The bullying didn't stop

I didn't make my daughter go to school the last two weeks of 5th grade

She missed out on the graduation ceremony and the walk to Dairy Queen

I'd seen enough of her crying; we went to Dairy Queen a different day, the two of us

On Election Day I followed the line as it snaked through the entranceway to the school,
 past the principal's office, down the opposite side hall near my daughter's fifth grade
 classroom

Every wall of the school was taken up with pictures of and quotes attributed to men of
 significance in American history

I could not find one female face on the walls of my daughter's elementary school

I remembered similar male faces and biographies on the walls of the school when
 my daughter had been a student eight years earlier, a similar lack of female
 representation

Earlier in the summer I'd been afraid to put a Hillary bumper sticker on my car

The whole town was for Bernie

I'd already had my car keyed for having a pamphlet from my daughter's university visible
 in the back window

I got my ballot and walked to stand behind a curtain to fill it in

I filled in the circle beside Hillary's name and then I looked down at the rest of the ballot

I'd never gotten around to checking out the website that explains the rest of the ballot

I looked for female-sounding names and filled in the circles next to them

I knew this wasn't the 'ethical' way to fill out a ballot but I didn't give a fuck

I voted for female Democrats when I could find them and when I couldn't I voted for female Republicans

Party line meant less to me than gender

I didn't give a fuck

I was tired of not seeing women's faces on the walls of elementary school buildings

I felt pretty good about my choices on my walk home

I wondered who the woman in front of me in line voted for

I didn't think it was Hillary

When I got home, I texted my daughter

"I'm turning into such a feminist," I said

I told her about my observations of her elementary school building, how there weren't any fucking women

"It's all I notice now," I said

"I know, " my daughter texted back. "I can't wait to vote!"

I went upstairs to write; I forgot about the election

It was 7 when I came back downstairs

"I've been in line an hour and 40 lol," my daughter texted. "I'm extremely determined rn," she said

"and so bored," she said. "just been meeting a ton of ppl in line lol"

"everyone's nice and they passed around a lot of pizza which helped," she said "being in your old school made me so angry at the school and at myself for not doing more when you were in fifth grade," I wrote in a text.

I added a hashtag feminist to the text before I sent it.

"Yeah lol I'm like suddenly super feminist," my daughter said

"I promised myself I wouldn't post politically on social media but then I got bored in line so I did lol," she said

"haha. what did you post," I said

"I posted on FB 'It's a beautiful evening to shatter the fuck out of the glass ceiling #imwithher'," she said

"so I'm a super feminist now," she said

"me too," I said

I smiled. I told her I was going upstairs to do yoga.

I added a hashtag superfeminist to the text before I sent it.

I took my daughter's lizard up with me

I did downward dog and runner's lunge and child's pose

I looked over at the lizard; she was lying with her arms back, palms up, under the table

I went back downstairs to check my phone; forty minutes had gone by

There was a photo of my daughter, smiling, an "I voted" sticker on her university fleece

"It was amazing!" she said

I immediately started to bawl

I was sitting on the edge of my bathtub

I'd never been this emotional in an election

I'd never fully realized the extent of sexism in America until a woman was running for president

My whole life I'd been in denial

I stared at the face of my daughter; so happy and excited

If Hillary didn't win it would be an insult to my daughter and my friends' daughters and to all our daughters

She would know how hated we are

I didn't want my daughter to know, I wanted her life to be different

She texted me that her professor liked her status about the glass ceiling

She said he had asked her earlier in the day to be his lab assistant next semester

My daughter was already more successful than I've ever been and I was so proud of her and I wanted the world for her

Or at least for a reasonable woman to be elected over an unreasonable man

I wanted my daughter to feel her vote counted

That our gender was truly able to accomplish what we worked hard for

She already worked so hard at her university

I tried to focus on the positive

I texted, "we need to remind ourselves Hillary has already broken a glass ceiling running for president"

I said, "we need to focus on the positive"

"I'm just excited that my first time voting in a presidential election was for a woman," my daughter said

"yeah," I said

"that's so exciting," I said

Acknowledgments

Thank you, Carrie Fisher.

Thank you, Andromeda.